Praying the Kingdom

Praying the Kingdom

Towards a Political Spirituality

CHARLES ELLIOTT

Paulist Press
New York/Mahwah

First published in Great Britain by Darton, Longman & Todd Ltd

Library of Congress Cataloging-in-Publication Data

Elliott, Charles, 1939–
    Praying the Kingdom ; towards a political
spirituality.

    1. Prayer.   2. Meditation.   3. Spiritual exercises.
4. Kingdom of God.   I. Title.

BV210.2.E39   1986   248.3   86-9461
ISBN 0-8091-2820-9 (pbk.)

Published by Paulist Press
997 Macarthur Boulevard
Mahwah, N.J. 07430

Printed and bound in the United States of America

Contents

CONTENTS

Preface

This book grew out of my experience of talking with groups of Christians in Britain, Ireland and the United States about issues of justice and peace. I learnt a great deal from those people and was constantly encouraged by their wish to work out an adequate response both to the facts of the Gospel and to the facts of the world about them.

In many conversations and discussions, however, it became clear that they were unsure how to do that, and, at a deeper level, were frightened of the pain and anguish that such a response might well engender. The temptation was to fall back on raising a little more money or writing yet again to their political representative ... They knew that, however sensible those activities might be, they were not in any sense an *adequate* response, and so they were left feeling frustrated, guilty and dissatisfied.

It would be absurd to pretend that this book 'solves' their problem. It does not. In it I try to show how those feelings of frustration, guilt and dissatisfaction can be used creatively, to take us deeper into the suffering of the world and its final outcome.

Two prefatory remarks, however, need to be made. First, prayer is a very personal business. What helps one person hinders another. There is no one method, no one route. God has made us different, and in our approach to him he does not expect us to ignore those differences. The approach I describe depends on the free use of imagination, fantasy, story and myth. It needs time and silence, recollection – and the courage to go on practising even when 'nothing happens'.

Second, a pre-departure warning, such as a Swiss guide gives as one stands, awkward, stiff, overweight and under-exercised, at the start of a climb. The guide usually tells you that it is going to be hard work, exhausting but exhilarating. That makes me feel even more awkward, stiff, overweight and underexercised and I start to plan strategies that will enable me to slink back to the car . . . This book is not hard work but it is none the less a *work* book. The temptation may be to read it from cover to cover, resolving to come back to the exercises, the 'work', some other time. Those who resist that temptation and put in the work that the exercises require will get a great deal more from the book than those who rush on. They will also, I hope, want to come back to the exercises and repeat them. It is often on a third or fourth repetition that new light dawns, illuminating whole areas of one's experience.

I have said nothing in the text about *preparing* for the exercises. Most people find it helpful, indeed some would say essential, to 'centre' before starting an exercise. This may be done in a number of ways – listening to one's breathing; feeling one's body limb by limb; or by noticing (but not dwelling on) the sounds that one can hear. The point is to create space – mental, psychic space – so that the deeper parts of oneself can come alive.

Chapters 1 and 2 introduce some spiritual problems that relate to praying for the Kingdom. Chapter 3 looks at some distortions of prayer. Chapter 4 introduces both the notion of story and some preliminary exercises. Biblically-based exercises are the core of the next three chapters. Chapter 8 reflects on corporate worship, and the last chapter relates prayer to living in the community and the nation.

Acknowledgements

I am grateful to Raymond Pelley for his permission to reproduce the story of Cathy; and to Alison Wynne and the
Resource Centre for Philippine Concerns for permission to
reproduce the story of Flora. The scriptural quotations are
taken from *The Jerusalem Bible*, published and copyright 1966,
1967 and 1968 by Darton, Longman and Todd Ltd and
Doubleday & Co. Inc, by permission of the publishers. The
quotation from *A Journey in Ladakh* is by courtesy of Andrew
Harvey and Jonathan Cape Ltd.

I am grateful to Susanne Garnett, Nadir Dinshaw, Gerry
Hughes s.j. and Pamela Gruber for reading the book in draft
and for helping me improve it. Its many remaining imperfec-
tions are my responsibility alone.

I am grateful to the staff of Darton, Longman and Todd
and especially to Teresa de Bertodano, for their encouragement, enthusiasm and professional commitment.

I am grateful to Gwyneth Goodhead who typed the manu-
script with speed, accuracy and never failing good humour.

And I am, above all, grateful to the many, many people
who have made this book by sharing their stories with me,
and by letting me learn from their wisdom.

To all who live the Kingdom
and bear its pain
I offer this book
in love and thanks

' . . . We imagine we want to transform ourselves and our
lives, but do we really? Do I? I am not sure.'
'You must go and find out. You must go and discover
whether there is anything in that world for you . . . Promise
me that you will go.'
'I promise.'
We stood in silence . . .

from Andrew Harvey: *A Journey in Ladakh*

1

Looking at the world

Christ told his disciples to pray for the coming of God's Kingdom. This book is intended to help his followers of today obey that command.

It springs from three observations. First, many Christians are shocked by the world in which they live, but are confused and perplexed about how to respond to it. Second, public and private prayer for the Kingdom tend to be, if not perfunctory, at least lacking the imagination and creativity that are brought to some other forms of prayer. Third, there are powerful psychological and spiritual forces at work which explain the poverty of prayer for the Kingdom in terms of the shock and perplexity I have already mentioned. If we can understand these and learn to transcend them, maybe we can revive our prayers for the coming of the Kingdom in a way that does justice to the great emphasis Jesus put on them.

This whole book is based on the premise that the coming of the Kingdom implies the transformation of human society – its politics, its economics, its personal, group, institutional and international relationships. The Kingdom is not some kind of extraterrestrial entity that will be superimposed on this world. Nor is it a process of 'spiritual' or 'internal' change that will leave the outer realities looking much the same. It is the liberation of the world we live in, know, touch, smell, suffer, from all that corrupts and destroys it. As we shall see, that certainly includes the liberation of the individual from all that corrupts her. But it goes far beyond that to the rediscovery of the real potential of the whole created order for that fullness of life in community that the Jews still call 'shalom'.

As they look at the world-as-it-is on the television, in the newspapers, on a meditative walk through the inner city,

1

what are typical reactions of typical people in the pew? I do not believe it is one of apathy or callousness or carelessness. If it sometimes looks like that – so that our critics rightly complain that the Churches are not notable for the lead they have given on some of the issues on which transformation is most immediately needed – I suspect that is to confuse symptom with cause. People may well be shocked, grieved, angry, revolted – but trapped. And therefore unable to react creatively.

That trap takes many forms. An engineer may be trapped by his job in a subsidiary of an arms company. A doctor may be trapped by his professional standards. A teacher may be trapped by her sense of responsibility to her students. A mother may be trapped by her care of the family.

Those are, however, pseudo-traps. They can be broken, with a lot of courage and a lot of pain. And some people, to their great credit, do break out of them. More generally, however, we need to go deeper to find the real causes of this sense of trappedness.

For most of us, it has two sources – a sense of guilt and a sense of powerlessness. It is these that I want to explore at some length.

But first a word of encouragement. To make it easier to follow, I shall write in crude and unnuanced terms. I do so not because I expect anyone falls into the trap I describe unreservedly: indeed many people who read this book will have transcended guilt and come to proper terms with their powerlessness. Rather I shall, in inevitably unsubtle colours, try to sketch a trap that many of us find a constant temptation. We may not fall into it – but we know it is there. Like a large terrier at our heels, it will give us a painful bite if we offer it the chance. The more aware we are of it, the less likely we are to give it that chance.

Guilt may take a number of forms. The most frequent and the most basic is guilt of the gap. I am so rich and she is so poor. I am well housed; they squat in a shanty. We leave more on the side of our plates than they have to eat. I go out to work every morning: he sits at home staring at television . . . These gross inequalities are so far removed from the spirit (and, for that matter, the letter) of both Old Testament and New that a primitive sense of dis-ease very soon acquires a biblical justification, a faith imperative. The gap is not just a fact of the world; it is a fact of God. Hence into the gap is released the dynamic of judgement. I am judged because I am overfed and she is dying of starvation – and I am judged harshly. Thus the guilt acquires a sharpness, a bitterness because it begins to erode the quality of my relationship with God – and the quality of relationship with myself. The downward spiral to anxiety has begun.

Guilt of the gap is, however, the crudest form of guilt as we look at the world. It is essentially static. Here am I: there is she. Once we start asking how this state of affairs has come about, what are the processes at work, two more levels of guilt are waiting for us. First, I am, in however remote a sense, in some way responsible for those processes: they are created, maintained and defended in my name and with my tacit approval. Second, I benefit from them, often at the cost of someone else. Let me illustrate.

The fact that I demand higher wages encourages mechanization and automation – and puts him out of work. The fact that I demand tax-cuts means that she is deprived of adequate health care. The fact that I demand cheap tea means that she, a tea-picker in, say, Sri Lanka, is under-paid, under-housed, overworked (for the months she has employment) and under-nourished.

These are all direct, relatively simple linkages – though arguably not as simple as I have represented them. We are all, however, caught up in much larger and more complex systems and relationships for which again we somehow feel vaguely responsible and from which we perceive some benefit. The nuclear arms issue is the most obvious example. There is a sense in which I have to bear my share of responsibility for the fact of the nuclear arms race. If – and it is an open question, but that doesn't affect the argument – if the existence and escalation of nuclear arms has in fact helped preserve a kind of quasi-peace in Western Europe over the last forty years, then I have certainly benefited from that. I am thus caught in the moral ambiguity with which we are all familiar. Even quasi-peace is better than outright war, but the moral indefensibility of nuclear armaments – and especially nuclear armaments with a first-strike commitment

– leaves me caught in a moral dilemma of which submerged guilt is a principal component.

The very nature of capitalism is in some respects a similar case. I see how far removed from biblical imperatives are the competitiveness, the acquisitiveness, the inner drives of the capitalist ethic, and all around me I see the corruption of that ethic in late capitalist society: monopoly labour slugging it out with monopoly capital in an uncreative, deadening trench-warfare that achieves nothing much for either side but leaves the social environment, especially of the poor, as battle-scarred as Passchendaele. Yet I am part of that. Almost in spite of myself – though I don't seem to resist very hard – I am caught up as voter, consumer, saver, investor, worker, employer in a system that too much denies and violates the finer possibilities of the human soul. I live in it and by it. I have not dropped out, copped out, or broken out. I depend on my pension plan being properly managed to protect me in old age. I compare models of cars, computers and cookers, searching for the best buy. I live on a State that, whatever party is in power, encourages and itself lives on a network of relationships and reactions that deep down I abhor.

That has taken us into the third layer of guilt. Consciously or unconsciously I reflect value systems and styles of thought (ideologies is too grand a word) that are inconsistent with both love of God and love of the poor. It is not only my unrecognized and unreformed racism, sexism and egoism, proper subjects of guilt as they are. I become part of a process whereby values, ways of looking at the world, mind-sets become embedded in our political and social culture.

Because I was on holiday in a remote village in Portugal, the first I heard of the Falklands War was when I found a copy of *The Times* in the nearest town. Opening it I saw a picture of the fleet leaving Portsmouth and the headline, 'Task force sets sail'. Avidly I read the front page and found myself caught up in the militaristic triumphalism that swept the British Isles in April and May 1982. It was longer than I care to admit before I saw my reactions in a finer light and came to recognize what had overtaken my country – and me.

Unless we are constantly and critically aware of our inner drives, we find ourselves reflecting and legitimizing values and attitudes that are far removed from those of the Kingdom.

As soon as we begin to become aware of how easily we are co-opted into the prevailing ethical standards; how hard we find it to withstand the pressure to conform, we glimpse a new level of guilt. We are salt that has lost its savour. We are yeast that has died. We are lights on a lampstand that have gone out.

Our guilt, then, is total. There is no way out of it. I may protest about the arms race, simplify my life style, eat lentils not meat, opt out of the consumer society, work in a co-operative, constantly examine my presuppositions and ethical assumptions. That may be good and worthy, but in the end I am caught. I am caught because I am human; and I am human in this society at this time.

The second jaw of the trap is powerlessness.

As I look at the world-as-it-is, what can I do about it? That is not only a rhetorical question. For the last twelve years, I have spent much of my time talking to church-related groups in Britain and the United States about issues of peace and justice. Two questions have become such familiar friends, I find it hard not to smile in recognition when they appear. One (which I shall ignore) is about population. The other, usually asked by a person of transparent sincerity and goodness, is: 'What can we *do* – here and now?'

Usually that question, and the discussion that follows it, reveals that most people think the honest answer is 'Practically nothing, and certainly nothing that will make a difference'. Their frustration is that they *know* that injustice and the denial of the Kingdom are, as it were, built into our political life and they can do nothing about it.

Let's have a closer look at different forms of powerlessness. I start with a homely example. I do so because it relates to a common experience and illustrates, in microcosmic form, some of the broader issues we shall have to come to.

Part of the year I live in a remote, secluded valley in mid-Wales. Only three families live in the valley year-round, and one of them, Phil and Trish Harley, lives in a caravan. They want to convert a neighbouring barn into a house, but the County Planning Committee turned down their application. Three reasons were given. It would increase the traffic on the road. Phil and Trish do not *need* to live in the valley. There is no provision in the County Structure Plan for increased housing in the valley. Phil appealed. The appeal was rejected. His friends wrote to councillors, the local paper, and met officials of the Planning Department. To no avail. Phil and Trish will have to leave the valley next year.

At least in this case it is possible to identify the people responsible for the decision. We can go and talk to them, expose the inadequacy of their arguments and show that we know what lies behind a decision that is incomprehensible in its own terms. That will not help Phil and Trish, but at least there is a recognizable process, managed by identifiable people, to whom we can make representations. Our power is overcome by their power, but we are not wholly voiceless or lost.

When one moves from the local, micro level of injustice to the national or international stage, those features disappear. Here are two, rather different, illustrations.

One of the many mechanisms by which the Third World is systematically impoverished (and I use the word systematically in its strict sense) is the terms on which multinational corporations acquire its raw materials, both renewable (like timber) and non-renewable (minerals). We may be able to find out the lumber or mining companies involved. We may be able to discover who are the directors. We may even be able to buy shares in major international companies and ask questions at shareholders' meetings. That is not a useless activity, but it does not address the basic question – who fixes the price of copper from Peru or Papua; of lumber from Sri Lanka or Ghana; of tea from India or Kenya? 'The market'. And who influences or controls or regulates the market? There the argument begins to run into the sand. There are two different sets of reasons for arguing that 'the market' is actually heavily loaded in favour of the industrialized countries, but this is not the time to explore those reasons. The key point for our present discussion is that the most powerful single mechanism for removing well-being from one group and bestowing it on another seems to be beyond the control of *any single group*. Producers do not control prices. Consumers don't. Despite much populist comment, in most cases multinational corporations don't. Each may have some influence, and that influence may be unequal. There is, however, no one single authority; no equivalent to a planning committee

6

which makes an unambiguous decision; no identifiable 'them' to whom one can talk or against whom one can rail.

The second illustration is from politics rather than economics. Let us agree that, at the very least, there is an ethical problem about the nature and level of expenditure on arms in both Britain and the United States. Now in theory we do know who is publicly accountable for decisions on MX or Cruise or satellite weaponry. And we elect them. Or some of us do.

These two short sentences could stand a lot of unpacking, but I want to make a rather different point. We know that no elected head of government is a free agent. Before he or she assumes office, pledges have been made, 'understandings' reached, trade-offs traded off. Politics is that kind of business, the business of winning sufficient support to keep your opponent out. And that means putting together coalitions of interest groups by agreeing to at least some of their demands.

In the United States, the defence industry has this process of influencing decision makers in the Legislature and Executive highly developed. There is not a Congressman or a member of the Cabinet or a President who lightly alienates the major defence contractors. In Britain and the rest of Europe, the power of the defence lobby is substantial, though still not above serious challenge. Yet the question remains: who *really controls* defence expenditure and therefore the major parameter of defence policy?

That raises a third form of powerlessness, one that is analogous to an issue we have already examined in the discussion of guilt. Leaving aside the activities of special-interest groups and their disproportionate effect on decision-making, those who make decisions are caught in their own mind-set, their own way of perceiving the world. If the key actors view the Russians as the personification of the forces of evil, whose only aim and intention is to secure world domination and annihilate every 'capitalist', they will react very differently from those who see the Russians as frightened ideologues caught both by the contradictions of their own ideas and by their geographical location between two potential enemies.

We are back with values, perceptions, world view. We may feel guilty that we are locked into them; we also feel powerless that we are unable to change them. And it is not, of course,

7

only the world view of politicians that we cannot change. (In theory, at least, we can change the politicians.) Politicians pick up and articulate aspirations, expectations, perceptions from our culture. In that sense, they are the volcanoes, of varying degrees of activity, which pass into the wider world the pressures and deeply buried matter of cultural formation. Of course, they give them their own shape and coherence. It is the raw material on which they work, however, that is ethically and logically prior. And, perhaps paradoxically, it is that which underlines our powerlessness. For we are part of that culture. As teachers or preachers; as parents or prophets; as people who pride ourselves on the breadth of our social contact, we are the stuff out of which culture comes. And yet . . .

Where conscious attempts are made to form or reform that cultural consciousness from within the life of the Church, it seems it is usually in an illiberal and individualized direction. The 'moral majority', associated with Gerry Falwell in the United States and Mary Whitehouse in Britain, represents a clear attempt to change the environment in which values are formed and political debate takes place. This is not the place to analyse those phenomena. I mention them only as examples of ways in which some Christians have sought to exert influence over the cultural environment; and to remind us that such influence may, in our judgement, have little to do with the real issues of the Kingdom.

I have called guilt and powerlessness a trap with a particular form of trap in mind – one of those spring-loaded, sharp-toothed man-traps that our predatory ancestors concealed under leaves or thickets for the discomfiture of their less appreciated neighbours and relations.

For there is a dynamism, a cruelty and a degree of concealment in the way guilt and powerlessness interact in our spiritual and psychological lives, which combine to make of them a trap of the most dangerous variety.

Dynamism first: guilt triggers a need to work out one's salvation. Leave aside, for the moment, the theological and pastoral dimension of that, and let's agree that most of us, once seized by a sense of guilt in any of the senses I have expounded it, seek to 'put it right', 'turn over a new leaf', 'mend our ways'. We want to *do* something – something fast, dramatic and effective. We want to purge our guilt. 'Don't flagellate; organize,' says one of the peace posters. And that's what we want; a sense that we can put right our past wrongs and live our newly discovered (or newly awakened) conscious-ness of our involvement in the sin and suffering of the world. Ideally we want to do something that will immediately and directly make a difference. Like the old aspirin advertise-ments, we want to be able to say, in the depths of our consciousness, 'Ah, that's better'. Hence the great success of money-raising devices that offer that dime-in/cure-out immediacy – adopt a child, sponsor a student, love a granny. However questionable such programmes are on the ground, they give the quick expiation of guilt we are looking for.

More reflective people realize that this stamp-machine approach to justice is scarcely adequate. For it leaves none of the roots of injustice touched. Adopt-a-child schemes merely produce one highly privileged child in a poor, under-privi-leged community. That is justice neither for the child nor for the community. Both continue to be held in a spider's-web of relationships, power-plays and assymetries that ensure their enduring misery.

We are back, then, with powerlessness. And that is the cruelty. We want to break out of our involvement in exploi-tation, in war and violence, but we find that whatever we do to achieve that is vanity. Vanity of vanities, all is vanity. So it seems as I demonstrate, or write letters to my political representative or newspaper. Nothing changes. Sure, I get polite letters back, assuring me that Mr Bloggs shares my concern and if only things were a bit different, he'd be only too glad to help . . . But things aren't different. They are as they are, and so Mr Bloggs makes unctuous noises and does nothing. He knows it and I know it.

And that burns me up. I'm left with my guilt unexpiated. And with my powerlessness and frustration unresolved. If I can face that honestly, I'm lucky – and unusual. More often, I don't face it at all. Either I pretend that what I have done is making a difference. We all know the readiness and smugness with which ecclesiastical assemblies pass reso-lutions condemning sin and sympathizing with suffering as though it made a fig of difference to either sinner or sufferer.

That lets me off the powerlessness hook. 'Look, we passed

eighteen really strong resolutions on civil rights in Central
America in the Lower Hogswash Deanery Synod last year.'
Or, more commonly, the unresolved tension goes under-
ground, into my unconscious, my soul, and there it plays,
almost literally, merry hell.

In the next chapter we shall have to look more closely at
how it does that. We shall there be led to find ways of dealing
with it at one level of consciousness. Chapters 3 and 4 will
clear the ground for a fresh onslaught at a somewhat deeper
level in chapters 5, 6 and 7.

2

Looking at myself

The most obvious effect of the failure to resolve or transcend the guilt-powerlessness trap is simply to turn off. The cop-out. Perhaps oddly, this is seldom made explicit or the subject of conscious choice by the individual. It is largely, often I suspect exclusively, a subconscious defence against the pain and anxiety that guilt and powerlessness engender. I can't cope with the agony of seeing my involvement in the suffering world; nor with the frustration of not being able to do anything about it, so I switch off. I am sometimes reminded of a trip-switch on an electrical circuit. When the current exceeds a given voltage, the switch is tripped and the whole circuit closes down. If it didn't, the cables would over-heat and the building would go up in flames. In that sense, the cop-out is a safety device – and a very important and health-protective one. It is not to be scorned. Nor, even more so, is it to be overcome, over-ridden, by huge efforts of will. To return to the analogy for a moment; I can go on using my strength to reset the trip-switch. The current will be restored and all will function normally. For a time, a short time. Quite soon, the switch will trip again, or I shall detect a strong smell of burning. Much more sensible to find out what is causing the switch to trip and put that right.

What form does the cop-out take? There is, of course, an infinite variety of particular forms, but the general form – the genus of which there are so many species – is an over-individualization of religion. Because I cannot cope with the pain of the world, I substitute myself for the world, and my religion, which will still surely not be painless, is focussed upon my relations with God, *my* state of grace, *my* progress (or regress) along the spiritual path. It is easy, and in some circles fashionable, to show how far removed such a rein-

11

terpretation of the nature of religion is from nearly all of the Old Testament, most of the Gospels, and much (but, emphatically not all) of the Epistles. Let us leave that to one side. What is important for us to grasp is that this exclusive concern for my religious state is pathological. It is a symptom of a sickness, and must be dealt with lovingly, gently and healingly. I need to be freed from the fear, from the overwhelming pain of the consciousness of myself-in-the-world, in order that I can live that consciousness in my spirituality and my activity. As long as I can go on running away from the fear and the pain, to a safe two-person ghetto inhabited only by God and me, run I will. Somehow, I have to find the courage to face the fear, to endure the pain, so that in both my prayer life and my active life I can take the world with ultimate seriousness. To do less, of course, is to deny both the majesty of the Creator and the reality of love incarnate. But watch me: I'll run to that ghetto, so warm, so comfortable, so undisturbed and undisturbing, given half a chance, as long as the pathology is unacknowledged and accordingly untreated.

A common way of trying to deaden the pain of the symptoms is hyperactivism. Some people, often unconsciously, seek to compensate for their guilt, pain, fear and powerlessness by a kind of manic activity that reminds the detached observer of nothing so much as a dance of Dervishes. I remember being summoned to a working dinner by senior officials of the British Council of Churches. We were sitting in what passed for a relaxed state of mind, politely sipping a weak cocktail, when in burst the dishevelled figure of a leading churchman. 'Sorry I'm late,' he panted. 'This is the sixth meeting I've been to to-day . . . And I have another after this.'

This absurd response needs to be seen for what it is. It is a defence against psychic forces that the immature soul can find no other way of resisting. It may have elements of pride and faithlessness – 'Aren't I worthy being so busy about the Lord's business?'; or 'The Lord really needs me to be doing his business' – but these are seldom dominant. Hyperactivism is much more an analgesic, a spiritual panadol. Taken in large enough quantities it will dull the pain. Better, it will make the pain quite unnoticeable because there simply isn't time or psychic space to feel the pain. Like most analgesics, however, it works for only a limited period. Sooner or later, the soul, like the body, cannot take any more and reasserts itself in some other way – by breakdown, burn out or crack up. And then the soul is in real trouble. At its weakest and most vulnerable to the pain and fear, the full force of the trap of guilt and powerlessness closes over it.

The individualization or privatization of religion and hyperactivism share another feature, which presents itself as another, separate, pathological reaction. Both privatization and hyperactivism often result in, or perhaps one should say manifest themselves in, a tendency to project on to others some of the unresolved conflicts represented by the concealed man-trap. Thus the highly privatized believer projects on to others stereotypes of carelessness, callousness, hardness of heart or undentable worldliness. The activist projects on to others, including the privatiser, stereotypes of gutlessness, timidity, failures of compassion or empathy. The activist is perhaps particularly vulnerable to this way of working, or pretending to work, his way out of the trap. He can project so much of his own unresolved guilt on to politicians, multi-national industrialists, financiers, the military, the police, 'them', that his own guilt becomes almost tolerable. If it wasn't for 'them', things would be so much better. Perhaps it is not surprising that there is little more chilling than an ecclesiastical assembly with an ideological bit between its teeth. The love of Christ gets short shrift when it may impugn ideological purity.

One further defence against the trap must be described – namely, that of substitution. A certain caution is necessary here, for the processes of substitution are not always obvious; and vice versa. What may look like substitution may not be anything of the sort. Nor is it obvious how far a conscious choice is involved: are we faced with a deliberate, wilful refusal to face the pain of the world, or an unconscious shrinking from that pain? I know that my resources of time and energy and spiritual input are limited, so I choose the object of my endeavours carefully, even prayerfully. So far so good. But when those endeavours are centred on the Home of Rest for Tired Pigeons or the Society for the Abolition of Fun on Sundays, what are the spiritual forces at work? Most likely, the need to find a substitute that is safe and manageable in that it does not raise in too sharp a form either jaw of the man-trap.

I sometimes wonder whether we do not use an excessive concern with the trivia of church life (in which I would have to include a lot of what passes for theological study) and the intolerance, intrigue and cruelty that often goes with it, as a defence mechanism against taking seriously either the fact of God or the facts of the world. How much more comfortable and psycho-spiritually handleable it is to worry about the state of the hassocks than the state of Nelson Mandela.

For a short time, I was loosely attached to one of the great bastions of Anglo-Catholicism in south London. It was true to every jot and tittle of the Anglo-Catholic revival, and therefore represented for me, used to celebrating the Eucharist in a schoolroom in the African bush, something of a change. I asked to be walked through the carefully choreographed ritual. 'Now do be careful, Father,' one of the curates admonished me, 'If your toe-cap is on the rug at this point, the mass may not be valid.' It is this confusion of shadow with substance that is one of the peculiar pathologies of Western and, alas, not only Western, churches. It goes, of course, far beyond the substitution that we are considering here and much of the time has nothing whatever to do with defences against inner pain and anxiety generated by the facts of the world. Another reason, then, for caution. Nonetheless, before we judge harshly, or at all, we need to be aware that some people all the time and perhaps many people some of the time find refuge in the trivial, the unimportant and even the absurd, not because they are, as people, trivial or absurd, but because they need insulation from the horror of the world and the glory of God.

To summarize the story so far: I have argued that when we face the facts of the world we are assailed by two psycho-spiritual reactions, guilt and powerlessness. These are extremely destructive in the way they interact and are accordingly likely to be associated with a number of defence mechanisms such as hyperactivism, stereotyping, individualization and substitution.

That is the bad news. The good news is that both guilt and powerlessness can, paradoxically, form a rich humus out of which prayer for the Kingdom can grow abundantly. To change the image, a central skill in most martial arts is to use the destructive power of one's opponent to one's own advantage; to make his energy work for his own defeat. A simple example in ju-jitsu is a quick, last micro-second duck before an oncoming opponent. It is too late for him to check his forward momentum. He trips over the squatting form of his opponent and takes a hard fall.

Can we, then, use the momentum, the spiritual force, of guilt and powerlessness, to our own advantage, to bring our prayer alive and make it a proper response to the facts of the world?

As we have seen, guilt takes many forms, but the most widespread is the sense of being caught up in a system that is intrinsically wicked and drawing benefits from that system. Two inner processes are then essential. The first is achieving a full awareness of the object of the guilt, the *prise de conscience*. As long as guilt is vague, half-acknowledged, shadowy, it will always constitute more of a threat than when it is fully explicated. In a heavy mist, a bullock may be taken for a dragon, or a copse for an army, as many a Welsh folk-tale will attest. Blow the mist away and the substance of the threat becomes clear. That does not mean the threat isn't real – even a bullock can give you the runaround. It does mean that it is defined.

That is easier said than done. Defining the nature of my guilt for the arms race, the international economic system, the international trade in food or pharmaceuticals is a highly complex and often contentious task. It may well be, then, that the last vestiges of mist, or perhaps quite dense skeins of fog, will linger on. We can never comprehend, for example, the intricacies and interplays of foreign and domestic policy that make disarmament impossible. But we can see, surely, that by stereotyping the Russians or allowing others to do so; by misdefining security and expecting to find it in military might; by contemplating the ethics of first use of nuclear weapons; by our very silence and connivance at the 'defence' decisions taken in our name – including the media intolerance of peace protesters – we are not guiltless. So much is obvious; it is common currency among those who think about these issues at all.

We need, therefore, to go deeper – deeper both into the world and into ourselves. We need to ask questions about our own aggression, our own defensiveness, our search for security and the sources at which we find it. So long as we think that strength guarantees security in relation to our family, friends and workmates, we are making the arms race inevitable. For, even in our most intimate personal relationships, we seek to arm ourselves and refuse to trust the security of love and respect.

Simultaneously, we need to see, initially in an 'external' factual mode, the implications of the arms race. The *full* implications will, of course, always be beyond us, but we can dimly perceive the scale of the misallocation of resources, the waste of brilliant minds, the institutionalization of fear and the legitimization of destruction on an inconceivable scale.

By 'marrying' our own inner drives and the way they work themselves out in our personal relationships to these wider implications of defence policy we begin to glimpse the ways in which we are personally implicated in, not only the arms race, but also in many of the moral breakdowns of our society, from the pursuit of violence to the acceptance of mass deprivation.

Before we see what we do with this 'marriage', this *prise de conscience* I want to work quickly through another example, because it is only when we can open ourselves fully to the pain of this *prise de conscience* that we can use its momentum creatively in praying for the Kingdom. As a rather different but no less skeletal example then, let us take the international trade in food. In northern Kenya people are dying for lack of food – the adults need energy foods above all else, the children both energy and protein. There is insufficient grain and milk in the country at a price that can be afforded by them or by the government. Why? Because for many years Kenya has followed a North Atlantic model of development, requiring very large volumes of imports. To pay for these imports, she has encouraged the production of tea, coffee, hard fibres, coconut and pyrethrum. Since the importing countries (of which Britain is one of the chief) have never seen fit to pay a price that reflects the 'real' human cost of production – while taking good care to ensure that the price of their exports do cover a comfortable standard of living for

16

those who produce them – Kenya finds she has to devote more and more land to grow export crops, and less and less land to basic grains for home consumption.

How am I involved in that process? In at least four ways. I complain at having to pay more for tea or coffee. I expect my wages to ensure me a certain standard of living, irrespective of whether I do that to peasants growing tea or coffee. I tolerate an aid policy that encourages export crops, and is grossly insufficient to meet Kenya's real needs. And, lastly, I connive at an agricultural policy in the developed world that produces surpluses which are too often disposed of in ill-considered and damaging ways that make it less likely that Kenya will produce enough food to feed her own population.

And what does all that respond to in my inner self? Essentially an egoism and greed that puts at the centre of my decision-making a drive to protect myself and those around me, not from want, but from forgoing what 'the world' regards as 'normal'. Raising prices of imports from the developing world; paying taxes to finance an adequate aid policy and to restructure Western agriculture – all these threaten, less my standard of living than my economic and emotional security. They call forth my defensiveness of what I have or have come to expect. I invest my possessions, my life style, my status symbols with more than a little of my own self-identity. To threaten them is to threaten an important part of me.

The 'marriage' here, then, is between these inner drives of security and self-esteem, the protection of the ego, on the one hand, and on the other, the shortage of food in a country, once seen as the great success story of East and Central Africa – a country in which, on one count, more than one child in five is clinically under-nourished.

How, we must now ask, can this *prise de conscience* enrich our prayer life? Is it not guilt writ large? Is it not the lower jaw of the man-trap with teeth freshly sharpened?

The gift of Christian faith is precisely that it enables us to transcend that guilt. That does not mean that we pretend it isn't there or isn't real or isn't loathsome in the sight of God and the sight of those who suffer as a result of it. It is all of that: yet we believe that, once we acknowledge what we can perceive of the full extent of our guilt, the love of God is such that we are forgiven, accepted, set free from the tendrils of sin and guilt that bind us and make us less than God created us to be. We are offered the possibility of 'new life in Christ', a quality of life no longer dominated by the failings for which we have asked forgiveness. This is, however, not an instantaneous, quick fix that makes saints of us at a stroke. Rather it is the promise of a new dynamic in our lives that allows us to confront the forces that make us and our world so different from what God wills for them.

I shall have much more to say about this in chapters 5 to 8. There we shall see how the whole biblical record can be read as God's longing to transform his people by the power of his love. He accepts us as we are, caught up in personal and structural sin as we may be, and offers us a quality of relationship that enables us to transcend the power of that sin in our own lives, and to engage spiritually and politically in the struggle to make ready for the coming of the Kingdom.

Critical readers will say that this account of the classical doctrine of atonement makes sense, if at all, only at the level of the individual's own spiritual development. It thus falls under the condemnation, it may be argued, of a privatized religion – which we have already condemned as a pathological reaction to the man-trap.

A reply consists of two arguments. First, remember the 'marriage' of my individual drives on the one hand and the socio-economic institutions and processes which they support on the other. On this account, a universal assault on those drives *is* an assault on the institutions and processes which exploit and damage the poor and the vulnerable. 'Structural sin' may well be identifiable as an entity, a force for evil, apart from the sinfulness of any one individual.

In the ultimate, however, with many time-lags and untidinesses, institutions and structural relationships do respond, slowly, hesitantly, with the grace and speed of a hippotamus with bloat, to the collective moral ethos. Change that and, in the very long term, you will change the world. Slavery, child labour and the cruder forms of racial discrimination are examples.

Second, the doctrine of atonement is essentially dynamic. By its very nature, it releases a new energy into the spiritual environment. *Because* I am, amazingly, accepted, forgiven, I

18

am more than ever determined that what was wrong, is wrong, will be put right. For reasons that we will come to soon enough, that will not catapult me into the kind of hyper-activism we have already discounted. It will, however, mean that I am not only more *aware* of my social impact; nor only that I am more critical of it; the 'new life' I am made capable of appropriating by degrees will be lived out *both* in the interior world of meditation and private prayer, *and* in the woof and web of my structural relationships. Precisely because I am set free of the guilt, the existential anxiety of my responsibility for the suffering of the world, I have greater energy, greater freedom, even greater joy to confront and confound the inequities and injustices of which I am part. It is in this sense that guilt, properly dealt with by acknowledge-ment and forgiveness, becomes a source of transforming energy.

Let us finally turn to the lower jaw of the man trap – powerlessness. How can that be made into a positive charge in our prayer life? Perhaps the answer is already obvious. For it is central. It is when we acknowledge ourselves as power*less* – as caught, trapped, unable to achieve any improvement in either our own inner lives or in the external forces to which they give rise – it is then that we become penetrable by the Spirit of God. As long as we imagine that the world can be changed by our activities, our good works, our energy, we substitute our effort for the power of God. That is as ineffec-tive as it is blasphemous. 'For thine is the kingdom, the power . . . ,' we pray, incidentally making a revealing and overlooked juxtaposition – and then, all too frequently, behave as if his is the Kingdom and ours is the power – and the glory too.

The power of God to transform, heal, renew and set free is grudgingly and half-heartedly accepted by most Christians at the personal level. Introducing a large group of senior ladies in the Church of England to some techniques of medi-tation, I was button-holed by one who was clearly somewhat upset. 'Your meditations', she began in a tone that confirmed my worst fears, 'Your meditations have done nothing for me. Nothing. Useless . . . until today, when you told us to let the Lord speak to us. He hasn't spoken to me all his life [*sic*], but today, he did. And do you know what he said? He said:

19

'For Pete's sake, grow up . . .' Now, what d'you think he meant by that?'

If we only half-believe that the power of God can change us, it is hardly surprising that we don't believe at all that it can change the politics of the world. And if we don't believe that, we are forced back either to total despair, or to fatalism – *que sera, sera* – or to hyperactivism.

By contrast, if we see prayer as a means of releasing God's power into the world, of enabling him to pour his transforming love into the critical centres of decision-making and activity, we begin to see paradoxically that we are not powerless at all. Our power to transform the world is God's power. That is hard to comprehend. Like so many spiritual truths, it is so simple that it takes some grasping. Certainly the mainline Churches have forgotten it or are afraid of it. I was asked to address the Synod of the Church of England on world development at the time of the publication of the Brandt Report. I concluded an analysis of the Report by saying that in my view, the proper response of the Church was one of, quite literally, prayer and fasting. Four days later I received an angry, stinging rebuke from a senior church official. 'I was very disappointed', he wrote, 'that all you could suggest was prayer. The last thing we want is to return to that kind of pietism . . .' When I enquired what help a major church-based charity gave its supporters to pray for the poor and the vulnerable, the answer was revealing: 'Oh God, we don't want people to think that all they've got to do is pray.'

Perhaps I can conclude this chapter with an image, an allegory, drawn from India, not a particularly poor part of India, true, but one which nonetheless has helped me to see the role of prayer in the coming of the Kingdom. I was flying over the Punjab. Great rivers wound, yellow-grey, across the limitless plain. Off these rivers and their tributaries had been cut irrigation channels; and off the irrigation channels, smaller and smaller ditches, until the whole plain was covered, like the blood supply in the human body. The last few yards of each ditch was controlled by a sluice or a simple mound of earth in the ditch. And each sluice or mound was controlled by one man or one family. As long as he opened his sluice at the right time and used the fertilising power of the water of the great river, the plain would be lush and green and rich. But if he kept the sluice shut, the rice would wither, and the plain would die – and so ultimately would its people.. We have the power of the sluice.

How can we use it?

3

Looking at prayer

When Jesus told his disciples to pray for the Kingdom, he assumed that they knew how to go about it. That may strike us as odd. After all, the disciples specifically and explicitly asked, not what to pray for, but how to pray. And Jesus answered by telling them to pray that the Kingdom, his Father's Kingdom may come. When we start to pray the Kingdom, what are we doing?

Most of this chapter is a demolition job. For it is easier to be clear about what praying the Kingdom is *not* than to define precisely what it is. Like the pork butcher looking for the lost sovereign in the salami sausage, let us slice away what is not relevant to our purposes.

There is a tendency deep in us all to assume that we know the shape of the Kingdom. We may admit under pressure that we don't know every detail, every hillock, but we are sure we know the main features of the topography. Secure in this knowledge, or rather pseudo-knowledge, we seek to impose it on God. We want a Kingdom where what we perceive to be Christ's values are given political expression; where mercy, forgiveness, harmony, mutuality, are given institutional and relational flesh. Our difficulty, often only half acknowledged, is that there is a great gulf between these values and their incarnation in the meat of political life. There is thus the danger that our prayer for the Kingdom becomes an ineffectual longing for the gulf to be bridged. 'If only the government would show mercy to the unemployed, O Lord'; or 'Let the State Department learn that harmony in the Caribbean Basin requires a total rethink of American policy on Cuba.'

From this kind of ineffectual longing for our present institutions and political mechanisms to incarnate certain values, it is but a short step to our prayer becoming little more than a political shopping list, a platform, a manifesto. 'May we have a more humane policy on employment; and that, Lord, means a proper balance of Keynesian and monetarist policies; more resources in training and labour mobility . . . Oh, and Lord, don't forget to do something about the exchange rate . . .' I burlesque only to paint up the absurdity. God neither needs nor wants a check list of policies that should be pursued in the preparation of his Kingdom.

There is here, however, a somewhat deeper point that ties in with some of the material of the last chapter. If we reduce the nature of the Kingdom to no more than a political manifesto we miss the whole point of the radical demand of the Kingdom. The politics of the Kingdom spring from fundamental reorderings of values, perceptions, world-views: without that deeper level of transformation the supersession of one political agenda by another is not only unlikely to be very effective: it is simply irrelevant. That may seem hard. 'How can it be irrelevant to the unemployed if policy changes so that they get proper training to enable them to get a good job? There's nothing irrelevant about that form where they stand.' No doubt: but if the policy change is brought about only to win votes or manipulate a given sectional interest, the unemployed will soon find that they – or some other vulnerable group – are again sacrificed to another political reality. If politics is played like chess, shoving pieces around a two dimensional board, the Kingdom cannot come. Yet when we reduce prayer for the Kingdom to a political agenda, we are making the Kingdom two dimensional despite the fact that the consistent theme of Jesus' teaching on the Kingdom is that it is multidimensional, involving liberating change at many levels.

This 'agenda approach' to prayer for the Kingdom contains within it another, somewhat analogous, difficulty. If I am sure that my agenda is God's agenda, I easily get impatient with those who stand in the way of its immediate implementation. At its crudest this degenerates into a political goodies and baddies charade, rather like poor Westerns, with the goodies in white hats and the baddies in black hats. This easy dichotomy is not only naive politics; it is bad prayer because it leads us to a more or less conscious writing-off of our political opponents. 'God rot Senator X because he's against civil rights.' However strange or perverse it may sometimes seem, God is not in the least likely to answer such prayer because he is not much into rotting people, even those who propound policies that are hard to reconcile with the Kingdom of the God of love.

None the less, most of us at some time in our lives come up against people who, in one way or another, represent or even incarnate a reality of evil that has to be withstood. While prayer for the Kingdom may not be a generalized curse on our political enemies, how does it react to the observed embodiment of evil in the political figures we encounter or are exposed to?

That there can be no compromise with the evil thus embodied needs no emphasis. As we shall see later in this chapter, the gospel accounts of the crucifixion give us some helpful guidance on prayer for the Kingdom, and in Jesus' encounter with the agents of evil, for him at that moment the incarnation of evil, we see how he dealt with this situation. 'Father, forgive them: they don't know what they're doing.' Jesus sees beyond them, to the deeper, larger reality that they cannot see. Blind, they cannot be blamed for the damage they do. As persons, they can only be the objects of forgiveness, unconscious as they may be of their need for it; resentful indeed of the gift as they may be.

So far from prayer for the Kingdom encouraging or even tolerating hostility towards those we identify as political foes, it requires us to see beyond the personalities involved to the reality of the evil of which they have become the agent. This is not simply a matter of 'hating the sin but loving the sinner': it is the process of detaching the individual from the forces of evil of which he has become the willing accomplice.

It is surprising – or, on reflection, perhaps it is not – how one's rhetoric turns and hits one in the eye. I wrote the paragraphs above secure in objectivity, the abstract removal from the immediate, where academics and poets are most comfortable. I then heard that the British government was planning to reduce its expenditure on overseas aid by £160 million, an amount equal to three times that which the international aid charities raise each year. The effect would be to reduce by nearly a quarter Britain's bilateral aid – at a time when over ten million people are at risk of starvation in the Sahel. Virtually every commentator agrees that the Sahelian/Ethiopian tragedy requires huge long-term aid commitments to boost food production, and yet the British government would now be seeking to reduce its already exiguous efforts in this direction. I know the ministers concerned quite well; we are on first-name terms and deal affably with each other across a half-acknowledged ideological gulf. I now have to live out the previous paragraph. While actively campaigning for their removal from office – with all that that means for them personally, in family terms and professionally – I have both to detach them from the actions to which they are party; to love them as men in and through that detachment; and to confront the world view (and the action that flows from it) which sees tax-cuts for the relatively wealthy in Britain as having a higher ethical claim than aid for the absolutely poverty-stricken in Africa. I do not find that easy – either loving the people so that I want *them* to see how far removed what they are doing is from the ethos of the Kingdom, or confronting the evil.

In the former, I am helped by a story from Yevtushenko's autobiography. He tells how, in Moscow in 1941, the streets were lined with people, mostly women, waiting for a great parade of German prisoners. The atmosphere of hatred was palpable. Nearly every woman had lost husband, father, brother or son, and now was their chance to desecrate the symbols of those who had killed their menfolk. The Germans came into view ' . . . thin, unshaven, wearing dirty blood-stained bandages, hobbling on crutches or leaning on the shoulders of their comrades . . . the streets became dead silent. An old woman pushed through the crowd, past the police cordon and, taking something from her coat, pushed it into the pocket of an exhausted soldier – a crust of black bread. And now suddenly from every side women were running towards the soldiers, pushing into their hands bread, cigarettes, whatever they had. The soldiers were no longer enemies. They were people.'

It is the second element, confronting the evil, that is harder, both conceptually and psychically. What does it mean in this particular case this particular morning? It means opening myself to the force of evil, not analysing it or describing it or attributing it: just standing in front of it, letting it break all over me, surge around me like a wild Orcadian sea . . . That, however, is too passive, though as we shall see at the end of this chapter, the passivity is critical and finally creative. Somehow, the puny resources of my spiritual strength, what some people call my 'soul force', have to be mobilized against this evil. It is no good hitting back at the sea, or at the wind that drives it. Yet the elemental forces of wind and weather have to be resisted by forces of love and inner capacity to transcend them. It is there that we meet both our own power-lessness and the power of God.

The confrontation with dis-incarnate evil is an ultimate spiritual contest. There is, however, a bogus version of this contest. Put at its crudest, this is the rehearsal before God of political grievances; the recital of a reverse shopping list of social or political shortcomings. 'Lord, we hate the abuse of power by the police; the overcrowding in our prisons; the inadequacy of our legal aid schemes . . .' This is neither a proper wrestling with evil; nor a costly opening of the soul to the love and power of God. At its worst it is a self-indulgent reinforcement of our own partialities which does nothing to mobilize our own or anyone else's spiritual energies. Indeed it can strengthen the power of both guilt and powerlessness and thus make real prayer the more difficult.

Perhaps an abuse of prayer for the Kingdom more common than disguised hatred of political opponents or the rehearsal of grievances may be labelled ideological buttressing. Let me illustrate. On my first visit to Nicaragua I was taken to a show-parish of the 'new' basic Christian communities, in a poor suburb of Managua which had been the centre of the resistance to the dictator Somoza. The present parish priest had been one of the first of the Catholic clergy to throw in his lot with the Sandinistas, and so it was no surprise to find liberation theology in rude health in this parish. What was more surprising, and to my narrow, WASP-ish mind distasteful, was the simplicity with which the Kingdom was identified with the Sandinist revolution. Even at the heart of the liturgy, priest and people hopped easily from biblical language to revolutionary slogans, and as easily back again. Prayer for the Kingdom thus became prayer for the success of the revolution. So far, so (relatively) good. What was missing,

26

however, was any acknowledgment either that the revolution may be less than perfect or that for it to succeed in any ultimate sense, transformation of individual, corporate and social consciousness would be necessary. In thus criticizing, I am not impugning either the sincerity of the people involved, nor the validity of their conviction that in the revolution they had seen the politics of the Magnificat come alive. They had, however, neglected the deeper truths of their own liberation theologians. Prophets like Guttierez and Miranda would never condone so simplistic a parallel between any earthly regime and the Kingdom.

I mention this example because we always see ideological buttressing more clearly when it is someone else's ideology that is being buttressed. How much harder it is to detect the same process when it is our own values and perceptions that are being affirmed in the process of prayer. My own tradition, the Church of England, is particularly vulnerable to this abuse of prayer for the Kingdom, not only because of its position as the established religion of the land, with all that that implies in terms of the monarchy, the House of Lords and the uncritical accommodation of the rich and the powerful, but also because of the symbiosis of the Church of England and English political and literary culture for at least 300 years. It is, for example, quite illuminating to examine the various liturgies of the Church of England from the Reformation to the issue of the current Alternative Service Book. One will find varying degrees of emphasis on prayer for the poor, the weak, the vulnerable. One will find no prayer for the rich, the successful or the aggressive. While there are prayers for the institutions of state – the monarch, parliament, the courts – there are no prayers that so much as hint at the terrible ambiguity of worldly power. On the contrary it is assumed that power is, and will be, used for the 'maintenance of religion and godly virtue'. The notion that the powers that be are to be confronted, challenged, chased back to a proper appreciation of their nature and purposes is to glimpse a world view quite alien to any prayer book ever adopted by the Church of England – or, for that matter, the Episcopal Church of the U.S.A. We should be careful, therefore, of the common assumption that it is only revolutionary priests in

Latin America who use prayer for the Kingdom as an ideological buttress.

No less destructive is the process by which prayer is used as the reverse of a buttress – a battering ram. Faced with a complacent, complaisant, lazy congregation, what young minister has not felt the urge to shock, to challenge, to offend? While it may be true, as a feminist theologian in the United States put it, that 'what the Church needs is a good kick in the rear', prayer for the Kingdom is not that kick. It may need that kick, or the shock or the offence, but it needs it as a precondition, as the *prise de conscience* of which we were thinking in the last chapter. Neither public nor private prayer is likely to come alive if it degenerates into disguised conscientization classes. Indeed those who use public prayer in that way need to reflect on what that habit says about their own power *vis-à-vis* those to whom they imagine they are ministering.

So far this chapter has been a list of negatives: of what prayer for the Kingdom is not. It is now time to try to pull together the few positive leads that have appeared and say what it is. To do so we need to go back to the discussion of the incarnation of evil, of threats to the Kingdom. Those are, in the majority of cases, threats to the poor, the marginalized, the vulnerable. For the Kingdom is for them first. The Kingdom is where earthly, ego-dominated values are turned upside down, so that the dispossessed possess; the have-nots have; the powerless achieve their ambitions; the outcasts are invited in. As Daniel Berrigan puts it:

> Heaven of such imperfection -
> Wary, ravaged, wild?
> Yes; compel them in.

The Kingdom is thus the triumph of the last over the first, of the humble over the proud, the ordinary over the exotic. Political spirituality is in part opening the inner self to the presence, the actual and spiritual reality, of these people, the inheritors of the Kingdom. It is being alive to them, welcoming them in, standing alongside them.

Is the language of that sentence metaphorical or actual? It is both. For it is only when we can, naturally and joyfully, welcome the poor and the oppressed into our community, our

28

homes, our family that we can, with integrity, welcome them into our souls. It is only when we stand alongside them on picket lines or dole queues or protest marches that we can claim honestly to stand alongside them at the still centre of our prayer life.

But is it as easy, as absolute as that? It is important to get the nuance right. I am well aware that I am very English, middle-class, slightly intellectual, shy, a clergyman . . . How can I genuinely *identify* with striking miners in South Wales or starving peasants in Mali? To welcome them into my home would be more embarrassing for them than for me. To stand alongside them would amuse them for its incongruity. Like Dr Johnson's dog, they would marvel not that I did it well or naturally, but that I did it at all. Try as I might, I cannot be other than I am. For better or worse, this is what God made me and I have trouble enough coming to terms with that, without trying to be something quite other.

And yet . . . And yet, unless I am moving towards that degree of empathy, of friendliness, of readiness to share, that would culminate in real welcome, actual standing alongside, there is little prospect of my being able to open myself to the poor at a deeper, more inward level. While we may, with proper caution, reject the absolutist position – 'in order to pray for the Kingdom, I must be on the picket line' – we have to be on the way to the state of consciousness that would make being on the picket line entirely feasible and appropriate. It will be surprising if that dynamism of consciousness does not involve, sooner or later, actually getting to know poor people *as people*. Sure we may find it hard to get to know African peasants or sweated labourers in Asia, but the call to prayer for the Kingdom is a call to know, to be acquainted with, the poor and marginalized in our own community.

The French language draws a distinction between *savoir*, to know a fact, and *connaître*, to know a person. Is it unfair to say that Christians are in general much better at *savoir* than at *connaître* when it comes to the people of the Kingdom? We tend to know the facts of deprivation, to know about injustice, exploitation, impoverishment. Trapped in our social classes, our literary ghettoes and above all in our ecclesiastical palaces, we are much less good at being acquainted with the victims of injustice or poverty. We do not, in general, find them in our churches. (And if they are there they feel they need to come in disguise – and that is perhaps the hardest judgement they can pass on us). The one social environment in which *savoir* ought routinely to be translated into *connaître* is usually one which insulates us most effectively from that translation.

I began to see some of the implications of that last Christmas. Being a 'spare' priest, I had been invited to assist in the Midnight Mass at one of our great London cathedrals. It was an awe-inspiring occasion: a huge and ancient church filled to capacity, superb music, rich vestments, stately liturgy, genuine worship offered in the best Anglican tradition. I have to confess it left me largely unmoved, almost alienated, even angry. I walked home, across the River Thames, back to the rather less fashionable area of south London where I live. Near my home are two shelters for the single homeless, a middle-class euphemism for methies and dossers. They were out in force that night. I was caught up in a weaving, wobbling human tide of sweating, swearing, singing, smelling men and women as they celebrated they knew not what, with an abandon and a welcome that the liturgy I had just left totally lacked. The liturgy had prayed, in beautifully crafted prose, for those people. Yet I could not help thinking that I was more likely to find Christ enjoying his birthday here than across the river. He, at least, would insist on *connaître*, while in the cathedral congregation, so edified by the beauty of holiness, we had been content to remain in the safety of *savoir*.

Prayer for the Kingdom, then, begins with a psychic, spiritual opening to the poor, which is likely to be dialectically related to an actual process of becoming acquainted with the poor. This inward opening to the poor is held in counterpoint to an inward opening to God, to his infinite love and his infinite power of transformation. It is thus a simultaneous standing in the presence of the poor and of God; a baring of the deepest parts of one's being to the stuff of the Kingdom and the King.

Put like that, it is too static, too immobile. One is standing in the presence of the victims of evil to expose them to the redemptive, transformative love of God. To use another language, one is adding one's own soul-force to the cosmic struggle of the love of God against the powers of darkness on behalf of their victims. Whatever language one uses, and all at this point are inadequate, there are four elements: the poor (a shorthand for all who suffer from the sin of their fellow men); the power of sin; the love of God; and you or me or whoever. At its most abstract, prayer for the Kingdom is confronting the power of sin in the love of God to liberate the poor.

Some will say that that is far too abstract. They will be wary of language like 'sin', and will want to particularize, to name policies such as apartheid, nuclear defence, colonialism, or labour exploitation. My difficulty about this is that it is a slippery slope which too easily results in us telling the King what his Kingdom should be like. At Mineral Point in Wisconsin, you may see a tapestry or sampler worked by the wife of a Cornish tin miner brought in to mine the local lead. The design of the sampler includes a cross, but the cross itself is unfinished. The old Cornish lady deliberately left it like that to emphasize that human comprehension can never finally contain the wonder and love of God. In much the same way, I believe, prayer for the Kingdom at its most powerfully meditative has to leave the detail unfinished. It has to depend finally and completely on the grace of God, and commit the supplicant and both the victims and the perpetrators of evil to that grace, that graciousness.

It goes almost without saying that that act of final commitment, with the purity of abstraction from the realities of everyday experience that it implies, is not easily achieved – any more than the depths of any meditative discipline are easily achieved. We shall return to this in later chapters.

The key point that needs to be grasped now, however, is that prayer for the Kingdom transcends the partialities of any political position we can define for ourselves. In that sense, it is dealing with ultimates rather than proximates, with eternal dimensions rather than temporal situations. That does not mean it ignores the real to concentrate on the unreal, or that it is so heavenly minded it is no earthly good. It is simply to insist that we recognize whose Kingdom it is, and that we honour the King.

I conclude this chapter by rooting this discussion in familiar biblical material. The choice of that material was suggested by a neighbour, a religious sister who specializes in spiritual direction. She often gives aspirants the exercise of imaginatively attending the scene of the crucifixion. She encourages them to enter deeply into that moment of history; to imagine the sounds, the smells, the light, the feel, the atmosphere; to look deeply into the faces of people standing round the cross; to watch and particularly listen to the Lord, as, struggling for breath, he heaves himself into a more erect position on the cross, defying the pain in his feet and wrists, to gain a lungful of air . . . 'Now,' she says, 'you are there: what do you do?' . . .

'And the extraordinary thing is', she tells me, 'that, almost without exception, men can't take it. They go away. They simply can't stand watching that intensity of suffering. So they slope off. Women can't stand it, either. But they are determined to save him. So they fling themselves at the cross to cut him free. Or they start rallying the crowds to take on the Roman soldiers. The one thing they can't manage in the face of such evident wretchedness is inactivity.'

The one person who did manage inactivity in that situation was Mary. She watched from a little way off as her son died. She entered his suffering as only a mother can and, we may assume, laid it alongside the conviction that he was no ordinary son. The reader may care to use that scene as meditative material before continuing to the next chapter – the scene of Mary watching the crucifixion.

It would be good to dwell on three aspects. First, Mary does not shrink from the horror of it. The blood is real blood. The fighting for breath is a desperate struggle for survival. The sense of abandonment is total. Second, she stays – and stays inactive, practically immobile. She does not try to organize a coup or lead a demonstration against the Sanhedrin, or abuse the cohort of soldiers. She stays and takes in the horror and the suffering. Third, we may assume that she is offering the whole event to God as she experiences it. The *whole* event. She is aware of the hypocrisy of the crowd, some of whom were healed by Jesus. She is aware of the self-righteousness of the Pharisees and religious establishment. She is aware of the callousness of the soldiers. She is all too aware of the timidity and gutlessness of the disciples and of how that, above all else, hurts her son now. And she offers all of that to God – quietly, silently, inwardly – while she is lacerated with all the emotion of a mother watching a favoured son, a son with the finger of God on him, die the cruelest death.

If we can enter into Mary's experience, we are beginning to know what prayer for the Kingdom involves.

4

Explanation and story

There is an old Punjabi fable about a man taking pumpkins to market in his little boat. He was an ambitious man and wanted to take as many pumpkins as he could. He loaded his boat to the gunwhale, and then kept piling on even more pumpkins. At last he agreed he had enough, so the loaders pushed the boat away from the quay. But stuck on the top of his pumpkin mountain, the man couldn't reach the steering oar. The boat drifted into the river currents, capsized and sank.

The temptation that many people face when preparing to pray for the Kingdom is that they overload their spiritual boat not with pumpkins but with facts. They think the more they know about riots in Sharpeville or sex-tourism in Thailand the more effective their prayer will be. It is a cross between the prayer wheel and justification by works: the faster we turn the handle with hard-won information, the greater will be the readiness of the Lord to hear.

That this is absurd hardly needs emphasis. God does not depend on us for news of what is going on in the world. If the temptation to overload with factual pumpkins must be resisted, so must the reverse temptation to shove off from the quay in an empty boat. It is important to know what can readily be known, what can be easily assimilated, what can nourish and sustain us as we enter the lonely, dark places where evil has to be faced and offered for transformation. To get this balance right – between not knowing enough and knowing far too much – is not easy. It requires an understanding of 'knowledge of the facts' so that factual information can, as it were, be cut down to size.

For facts by themselves are useless and/or meaningless. What does it *mean* to say that income per head in Nicaragua is five times that of India; or that more money is spent on nuclear research than on research on preventable diseases? Facts only come to life when they are used – to explain or to guide to action. They are given coherence in theory, paradigm or decision-rule. But to construct a theory, you need to choose your facts. That does not mean that theorists deliberately exclude facts that do not fit the theory, but it does mean that they look at a very partial piece of experience, a very limited array of facts. This may enable them to produce a theory that 'fits the facts' quite well: but it may not fit *all* the facts or all the facts observed from all perspectives.

Physical science is constantly running into such problems, as developments in the theory of matter over the last twenty years so readily attest. More powerful microscopes and electron accelerators have radically changed both the nature of the facts to be explained – matter is not what we once thought it was – and the nature of the theories that will cope with those facts. Now scientists are increasingly aware of the provisionality of both 'fact' statements and 'explanation' or theory statements.

In much the same way, social scientists have become more conscious of the transitoriness of problem, fact and explanation. Perhaps more than that, they have become exceedingly cautious of prescriptions based on 'explanations' of social 'facts'. The exportability of Westminster-types of parliamentary democracy; the desirability of high rates of economic growth; the superiority of Western models of treatment of offenders; the inevitability of urbanization are four very different areas where fact, explanation and prescription have all changed substantially over the last twenty years.

It is precisely this time-boundedness of theory, and the dependence on theory for the meaning of facts that should encourage us to sit fairly lightly to fact and explanation as we prepare for prayer. For what may look 'factually certain'; or what may be 'a thorough explanation' may, in an ultimate sense, prove to be simply wrong.

Since we can know neither fact nor explanation in any ultimate sense, while the process of praying the Kingdom is precisely the process of confronting ultimates, we should not waste too much time and energy on equipping ourselves with an encyclopaedic knowledge of the subject of our prayer.

Know enough, enough to nourish and sustain and focus, but sit lightly to what is known since it is as likely to obscure as it is to reveal.

So far we have been considering the kind of knowledge that politicians, social scientists, journalists and historians are interested in – factual knowledge given coherence by incorporation in some kind of narrative or explanation. There is however, another kind of knowledge, namely subjective knowledge. By that I mean knowledge of how people think, feel, suffer in a given situation. This is knowledge of their *story;* their account of what it means to be them, particular human beings, in a particular context. An example will make the point.

There are available many analyses of apartheid: its legal framework, its economic causes, its social effects, its political implications. They make sombre reading. They describe, however, an outward reality. That is not unimportant or irrelevant, but most people find more nourishing the inward reality of apartheid as experienced by those who suffer its effects. I was invited to attend a grand conference on poverty in South Africa at the University of Cape Town. Hundreds of social scientists, lawyers, politicians and community workers attended. We read to each other over three hundred papers of varying degrees of sophistication and abstraction. Far and away the most effective 'paper', however, was the simple autobiography of an old Zulu man who had been forcibly relocated. He told his story with quiet dignity, without bitterness or rancour, as if this kind of behaviour was what one had to expect from white upstarts. That story, with all its bathos, lives with me still.

'Aha,' cries the Afrikaner, 'How d'you know he was telling the truth? I'll bet it was a pack of lies designed to make political points or win the sympathy of you liberal foreigners.' The Afrikaaner is more right than he knows. The interesting question, however, is not 'whether he was telling the truth' in a scientific sense (that we, and perhaps even he, will never know) but whether he was creating a life-giving myth or a life-destroying one. To call a story a myth is not to prejudge its literal scientific truth. It may or may not be literally true or empirically verifiable. What makes it a myth is its power to enter and form the consciousness of the hearer. This power is related to its ability to represent a reality larger than itself, to act as a symbol of a truth that transcends the limits of the subject of the myth itself. Myth thus points beyond itself to a realm of experience, even of exploration, that forms the stuff of consciousness.

Clearly the ethical value of myth is thus an open question. Hitler's regime in Nazi Germany survived on a diet of myths of the Herrenvolk, just as Rastafarian cults in the West Indies survive on myths of the 'return' of Haile Selassie. Those are examples of baseless or false myths. The strength of nationalism in Central and South America, however, is explicable only in terms of the emotive power of 'true' myths about colonialization and neo-colonialism. The difficult and costly search for an African socialism in such countries as Tanzania and Ghana was inspired and kept alive by the myth of a pre-colonial African culture marked by interpersonal co-operation and harmony, relative equality, respect for the elders and the weak, and the honouring of reciprocal obligations. (How far this myth is true is a complicated and much debated issue which cannot detain us here: what is relevant is its ethical, and political, load.)

We thus have three essential features of myth: its power to form consciousness; its truth-base; and the moral direction in which it points. Myths that do form consciousness; that are based on, or reflect accurately; true propositions about the world, that have a moral direction that is consistent with the Kingdom – such myths are the sustaining fare we can use in prayer for the Kingdom.

We are, however, immediately faced with a number of difficulties. How do I distinguish between a myth that is 'true', in the minimal sense that it does not mislead or misrepresent reality, and a myth that is dangerous because it leads one away from reality? And how do I recognize that the moral direction of a myth is consistent with the Kingdom when I am told to be careful about projecting my agenda on to the Kingdom? These are real and important questions, as the tragic history of the Church in South Africa, Germany, much of Latin America and, one is obliged to add, the USA and the UK, so readily attests. In each case, destructive myths have played a role in leading the Church from genuine prayer for the Kingdom. The myths of the Voortrekker, the Herren-

37

volk, of national security, of the moral superiority of capitalism – these have all been absorbed into, and then helped
misform, the collective consciousness of the mainline
Churches.

Is a myth 'true'? To repeat, the question is not about the
literal truth of the story, but about the underlying vision of
reality reflected in the myth. We need then to check our own
vision of reality against that of the myth. That is not as simple
or as unambiguous as it may sound, not least because both
'visions' are likely to be apprehended only uncertainly. Nor,
perhaps paradoxically, is it necessarily true that the more I
know about a subject, the clearer my vision of its reality
will be. Indeed, I may well come to see how complex and
multifaceted is the issue the myth addresses. However careful
we are in our checking of the myth against the 'facts', we
shall still finally have to make a leap of faith, of commitment.
'I don't *know*, but I am ready to believe that this myth, this
story, does not lead me away from the truth.'

And is the myth consistent with the values of the Kingdom?
Although we shall feel more confident about answering that
question when we have looked at some of the biblical material,
there still remains for us another leap of faith. We shall never
know what the Kingdom will be until it is here, but we do
have sign-posts, indications, hints that invite us to commit
ourselves to myths that promote mercy, generous dealing for
the poor, harmony, justice and peace. We have to be as sure
as we can be that the myth is in tune with those values, and
then make the leap of faith that commits us to it.

Selecting our myths, then, is no easy or random task. We
can learn something from the epicure. He may not know
every wine on the list, but he does know a reliable shipper
when he sees one. In the same way, we can choose our
myths from reliable sources. We can put those sources into a
hierarchy. The first is our own experience. For that there is
no substitute. If we grow towards the openness towards the
poor that we were discussing earlier, we shall find a rich
source of sustaining myth, not only in the stories of the poor
themselves – it will take us some little time to learn to hear
those, for we will approach the poor with the expectation that
they have little to tell us and that whatever they have to
say will be said inarticulately – but much more in our own

observations of and relationship with the poor. Without exploiting the poor to generate myth for our benefit, we can become sensitive to the present moment in their company, and unfussedly store away small incidents, looks, nuances, silences, exchanges that have, for us, the power of myth.

The second level of the hierarchy is stories of people we know and respect. We cannot hope to have such a wide direct contact with the suffering of the world that we can furnish ourselves with an adequate menu of myth. We must depend on others to expand the boundaries of our experience. At its best, the Church enables that to happen. It brings together people from the local community who can share their experiences, pool their myths. More, it can bring people together across cultures to hear (not just listen to) each other. By that I don't only mean transcontinental exchanges: I mean exchanges across local cultures. The Churches in general, and the Anglican Church in particular, are astonishingly reluctant to acknowledge the potential of story. Here in south London, for example, in a notoriously 'difficult' parish in a riot-torn racial melting pot, the Church is only now beginning, very cautiously, to encourage the various cultures to share their stories. And the value of those stories to sustain prayer for the Kingdom is seldom recognized. When it does happen, the effect is electric. Prayer comes alive. Consciousness is transformed. You can almost feel the Spirit beginning to move in a congregation.

Romy Tiongco works in the Philippines, organizing very poor peasants to improve their living standards and resist those who oppress them. A former priest, he is a gentle, courteous person, a skilled communicator. He spent a week with a group of congregations in south-west England. He could have harangued them, or given them a heavy dose of liberation theology or political analysis. 'He was content just to be with us,' said someone from the area, 'and share a little of himself. Now we shall never be the same.'

The third tier of sources, and in every way the least satisfactory, is the media — from the printed word to the film or television report. Because we have largely failed to develop our own experience and that of our community as sources of story, we have become over-dependent on the media, and therefore trapped by the questions of truth and moral direction we were looking at earlier. To some extent they can be handled by the same technique – know the shipper. Trust the Episcopal Conference of Latin America more than the State Department or the *Daily Telegraph*. Yet the basic difficulty may not be questions of verification or ethical consistency: the real problem is more likely to be that of effectively internalizing the 'right' media stories so that they acquire the power of myth.

To summarize, I have argued that fact and explanation, the 'natural' sources of prayer for the Kingdom, are not to be ignored, but nor are they to be allowed to hog time and energy, primarily because they endow the subject with a specious objectivity, and can therefore close off parts of reality to which we should be open. I have suggested that myth and story, words I have tended to use interchangeably, are much more useful sources, but that they too need to be handled with some care. Some myths are more in tune with the Kingdom than others; some therefore are more helpful in putting us in tune with the Kingdom than others. I want to end this chapter with a few myths I have found helpful, and then consider in what way they have been helpful. I shall give examples of the three varieties we identified a few moments ago.

First, then, here are two stories from my own immediate experience.

I was in northern Namibia, in the so-called 'operational area' where the South African Defence Forces were fighting the South West Africa People's Organization. There was a huge military presence, with heavily defended camps of the SADF every few miles along all roads of any consequence. The local inhabitants were frightened, demoralized, aching for peace and freedom from fear and oppression from both the SADF and SWAPO. But the most frequent complaint was the oppressiveness of racial stereotyping, of the brutality – physical, emotional, spiritual – of rank racism.

Each morning foot patrols of the SADF moved along the roads with hand-held mine detectors, clearing away any devices planted by SWAPO overnight. These patrols were mounted by all-white detachments, usually very young drafted men. I came upon one such patrol early one morning, quite close to the Angola border. I was in the front seat of a truck with two Africans.

We crawled behind the foot patrol for a mile or two, as the heat rose, and with it the dust. Suddenly, something snapped inside a young lance-corporal. He was right in front of the truck. Turning for the first time, he saw the driver and the African in the middle. He swung his mine detector, with its heavy metal head, at the windscreen of the truck. In the split second it took the instrument to travel through the air, I caught a glimpse of his face and, through its transparency, of his soul. Hatred, contempt, anger were there in their purest essence. At the very last second, the soldier caught sight of me on the far side of the truck. Instinctively, he deflected the mine-detector so that it struck the windscreen pillar and fell harmlessly to the road. His face again revealed his inner torment: guilt, fury, frustration, trappedness and a desperation to be released from his present predicament. For me he is the symbol of the misery of white South Africa.

Most people know the bare facts of El Salvador: a right-wing Government, protecting the economic and political interests of a small élite and its clients, locked, with American assistance, in a futile struggle with a broad coalition of Centre-Left groups in a civil war that neither side can finally 'win'. In the meantime, much of the rural civilian population of El Salvador is caught in the middle. Many people flee from their villages and seek shelter in the small towns. These are sometimes attacked and captured by the 'guerrillas', and are then bombed by the government forces. It is thus a very limited sense of security that such towns offer to the refugees.

When I last visited San Francisco Gotera, the neighbouring town was being bombed and refugees were crowding into the three small camps run by an international Franciscan community of men and women. The community welcomed us, shared a simple meal and some of their recent experiences. Matter-of-factly, it came out that there was shooting outside the house every night, so that an unbroken night's sleep was beyond anyone's recall; that the previous week the superior of the community had been issued with a death threat by the local army colonel, a close friend and army colleague of the diocesan bishop; that none of the community expected to get

41

out alive, but none wished to leave; and that in that decision they had found a depth of love, peace and meaning that years of devotion to the religious life had not won for them.

After lunch they took us round the camp. They cuddled the children, joked with the men looking for relief from pain in the bottle, held the hands of the dying, prayed with the desperate, helped dig the latrines. It was hard not to see the love of God incarnate in that miserable camp.

They took us to the landing strip and we waited, in the gathering dusk, for our light plane. Lying in the coarse cool grass, I talked to one of the nuns and discovered common friends and places. Perhaps inevitably, the conversation touched depths in each of us, homesickness and longing in her as she looked back, tenderness and compassion in me as I looked forward for her.

The plane arrived. Farewells had to be rapid. A curfew was already in force, and to break it was dangerous. Suddenly I found the nun in my arms, sobbing like a child and, like a child, needing the comfort of touch and warmth and soothing sound. Slow as ever, I saw at last the reality of fear with which she and her community lived day by day.

For a story culled from someone else's experience, I take an extract from an address, preached at her funeral by her father, in memory of Cathy, a girl of nineteen. She had been drowned during a family holiday.

'I remember her at fourteen. To understand Cathy you have to realize that she had sensed at a very deep level that the energies to create a more just and more human world were coming especially from the poor, from indigenous peoples and from women. In New Zealand this meant for her an identification with the Maori people. Some of her closest friends were Maoris. Not only did she immerse herself in Maori language and culture, she also joined in the struggle to regain the land which the Maori people had lost to the white settlers. At Bastion Point (quite close to the college) there is some disputed land on a beautiful promontory looking out over Auckland harbour. The developers wanted to get hold of it to build expensive, desirable residences. The local Maoris, the Ngati Whatua, organized an occupation of the land. Cathy went and camped with them. In the very early morning the police arrived with arc-lamps, batons and riot-shields, paddy-wagons, the lot. They warned the people that anybody still on the disputed land one hour later would be arrested. Some left. Cathy, a few pakehas (whites) and the Maoris stayed where they were and were duly arrested. She spent the rest of the day in the Central Police Station in Auckland. To survive she went and did yoga in the toilet; and then she sat trying to persuade one of the policewomen to change sides. Some of the Maori activists graciously took it upon themselves to stand with her in that place. And many Maori people I have spoken with were deeply impressed with Cathy and knew that she was on their side. One of the telegrams Jo and I received comes from three Maori activist groups and it reads: 'Sorrow at loss of spirited fighter of Bastion Point. Kia kaha. All members of the family Arohanui.' Cathy's courage and integrity that day did not go unnoticed nor will it be forgotten. It was out of this kind of experience that she wrote her song, 'Crazy White Man'.

'At this point in Cathy's life she went through what was truly a life and death crisis. I can only hint at what happened. All at once – and this was before her fifteenth birthday – she rejected everything: school, family, her old self, religion, her class and racial background – the lot. The day she ran away from home she left a note in my bed which said: "Dear Raymond. Please don't send the police after me. I want you to trust me because from now on I'm taking responsibility for my own life." Jo and I took her at her word and for two weeks we didn't know where she was. But despite our anxiety we managed somehow to trust and support her. In the year or so that followed, which was spent in an alternative life-style community, in a time wandering around New Caledonia/Noumea, in a bach at Piha, and in Auckland, everything went wrong – outwardly. Cathy's sense of identity collapsed. She felt suicidal and disoriented. Her physical health broke down to the point where her life was at risk. During this time she lived with people who were black or brown and mostly of her own age. However, what from a white, middle-class standpoint looked like a social and psychological disaster was in fact for Cathy a time of revelation and exploration of new life. The values from her background which she outwardly rejected were at another level

43

being radicalized, recreated and acted out. It was as though she gave her old life away so that she could receive a new life as a gift. In the moon and the stars, and in mother earth, she discovered a source of healing, empowerment, goodness uncontaminated by the corruption and violence of society. It was as if she had in her own very costly way discovered for herself the overflowing grace and life of God pulsating through the universe.

'Is there any way finally of explaining Cathy's extraordinary strength and vitality? I suppose in the end I have to make use of biblical language and categories to begin to do justice to Cathy. It was as though she had given her life in order to find it. Or it was as though she had been driven out into the wilderness by the Spirit of God there to wrestle with the demons of our time. In that life and death struggle she won for herself the vision that in her writing, her art-work, her songs, and above all in her life she was strongly articulating and acting out. Like one of the great mythical heroes of the Pacific, Maui, it was as if she had gone fishing with a great bone hook baited with her own blood and pulled up a whole new continent, beautiful, fertile and teeming with life.'

My final example of story or myth is from a collection of womens' testimonies from the Philippines. Edited by Alison Wynne and published by the Resource Centre for Philippine Concerns in Hong Kong, it is called 'No Time for Crying'. This is (part of) Flora's story.

'I worked in a hacienda of seventy-two hectares with seventy workers. In 1972 the workers elected me as their leader. We heard on the radio that all workers should receive a minimum wage of 7 pesos [US 95cents] per day and yet we received only 3 pesos [US 41cents]. We decided to take our complaint to the local constabulary. When we arrived the commander told us to go to the National Labour Relations Commission. We went there, thirty-eight of us, asking for the minimum wage, medical benefit and other things the government said we should receive. A hearing was set for a future date, then it was postponed and scheduled for another time, and this treatment went on and on for months. During this time the union-member workers were locked out and had no work. I was surprised that the management locked us out simply because we complained and asked for the benefit which was ours by government decree. We were very angry because we had no money and our families were going hungry. Even when we received the back-to-work order the hacienda owner would not take us back.

'One evening, all of us who were out of work discussed what we could do. We decided to go to the owner of that hacienda and explain what we wanted. We simply wanted work so that our children would no longer be hungry. He told us, "Go away. You are rebels." That is how we are regarded when we are no longer ignorant of our situation as workers.

'We travelled from one hacienda to another, but could find no work because we were known to be union members. Sometimes we would go secretly to a hacienda to organize the workers and talk with them in the evenings so that they could learn their rights. One time two people were sent to tell me, "Stop your work or you will be stockaded." But I ignored the threats.

'The union has taught us our rights. Before that we didn't know. The union taught me my rights and also how to teach other people their rights. Many of the women in the hacienda never went to school beyond the age of nine years. The families were poor and parents would tell their children to leave school and go to work in the fields so that there would be enough money to buy sufficient food. So the children would stop school and go to work to help earn money for the family. In this way workers have no chance to grow by realizing their oppressed situation. Our grandfathers died as exploited sugar workers, our parents are exploited sugar workers, and we are continuing the pattern.

'During the milling season, when there is too much work for the permanent sugar workers to handle, the hacienda takes on *sacadas* (migrant sugar workers). They are the ones who really suffer from exploitation, especially by the man who handles their contract on behalf of the hacienda owner. The *sacadas* work in teams by themselves, cutting and loading the sugar cane for milling. The permanent workers tend to regard the *sacadas* as being inferior people. Generally speaking, the *sacadas* are despised by everyone and I feel deeply sorry for them in their sufferings.

45

'In the Philippines we have problems because we have no unity. People feel that they have their own culture and their own problems, and they don't want to be burdened further by the problems of others, failing to realize that the problems are the same. No work, no food. That is the basic problem. There is no money to buy rice. A major problem in the sugar industry is that sometimes you work for only four months of the year, and you cannot support a family for the remaining months. Many girls work as servants for rich people, and children will go to the mountains to help harvest the rice in the hope of receiving a little money or food.

'I hold district meetings of the sugar workers in several areas once a week. We sit and talk, and plan how to solve the problems which arise among the workers. Every time I go to places for meetings I am harassed. The police follow me all the time, but I am not afraid. I give thanks to God that I can still do my work and help people to stand up and feel more human. Now that I have discovered my rights I am determined to pass on this knowledge to others. The minds of the workers are very closed. The workers are afraid to stand up for themselves. I want all of them to say, 'I am a person, like you. These are my rights that I am demanding.' We must unite to achieve our demands. We cannot do it alone because of the forces of oppression which are against us.

'Now the hacienda owners are becoming afraid. They say to me, "Why are you disturbing my workers and causing trouble?" Before the workers were afraid of the owners. Now the workers are getting strong and the owners are becoming afraid.

Here, then, are four stories, very different in form, content and inner significance. All four, however, can sustain prayer for the Kingdom. Let's see how.

¶Start with the story of the young soldier in Namibia. Read it again. Imagine you are there, sitting in the truck. Watch the soldier on the right. He turns round wielding the mine detector. Look at his face. Freeze it. Look again. . . . What do you see there? Don't analyse it. Feel it. Let it enter you. Experience all the anger, the murderous hatred that he feels. . . . He feels it for your friends on your right. He feels it for anyone black . . . Now he sees you and he deflects the detector. Watch his face again. . . . Feel his confusion and his frustration. . . . Watch. . . . Do you see him just perceiving, however dimly, the absurdity of his own reaction . . . and of the whole situation?

Now you can experience him as a human being. . . . Poor little devil, what a muddle he's in. . . . Try to speak to him . . . to show him your love.

Alternate between the perception of his murderous hatred . . . and him as a lovable human being. . . . That's hard. You may have to work on it, or come back to it. . . . If you can manage it, offer the hatred and the anger to God. He can deal with it. . . . Now offer that poor soldier as an individual. . . . And now as a representative of all who are corrupted by racial hatred, whatever their colour. . . .

You may well have found that difficult. And it may seem to get little easier even after three or four repetitions. Don't be alarmed, or think this is not for you. (You may, of course, find other ways of praying more helpful. That's fine. There is nothing exclusive or unique about the methods we shall be exploring in the rest of this book.) All prayer is hard work, and you may need to practise 'freeing' your imagination. . . . Most people are surprised how soon it does 'free up' and how rewarding that can be. And that it is based on *my* story, a story that is part of my experience. To you it is just a written story. That is why personal experience of injustice and a personal acquaintance of those who suffer it are likely to reap not necessarily 'better' stories – much of our experience is humdrum – but stories that can more adequately sustain us.

¶Let's try the second story. Read it through a couple of times, and enter imaginatively into the three 'scenes' – the meal and the conversation that went with it; the tour of the refugee camp and the 'style' of the Franciscans with the refugees; the conversation at the landing strip. When you have entered this material imaginatively so that it is 'yours', go through the camp again and give thanks for every gesture of love, compassion and mercy that you notice. If you look, you'll be surprised how many you see, not only from the Franciscans, but among the refugees themselves. One is helping another fix some fertilizer bags as a roof to his shack. An old woman is comforting a neighbour's child. A young man is replacing a washer on the one communal tap. . . . Give thanks for every such act that you see . . . and then hold up all such acts as symbols of every situation of despair and desperation where compassion, sharing, mutuality, gratuity are alive. For the Kingdom is built in such places; and such acts are its bricks.

Then go out to the landing strip. Talk to the nun (or, if you find it more natural, to one of the priests) about herself, her family, her life. Talk to her about her inner life, and especially how the present situation, the imminence of death or worse, has brought alive her prayers and her sense of joy in community. Experience her as a person – a whole, many-sided, lovable but flawed person, not as a cardboard cut-out in a wimple. Enjoy her company. Laugh with her; poke fun at her; let her pull your leg. . . . The plane has arrived. You get up to go. And there she is, sobbing, trembling with the fear she usually manages to repress so well. . . . Hold her tight. . . . Let her cry. Let her cry enter deep into you. . . . Don't try to control it, box it in. . . . Be as open to it as you dare, even though it hurts.

Now offer it to God. He knows it at first hand. Gethsemane made it very real. It's the fear of anyone who takes the risk of love of others, of giving themselves totally for the poor, the frightened, the downtrodden. Offer it all – and offer all those who today know that fear.

Now we move to Cathy. Notice again the difference in form of the story (or stories, since there are two separate incidents). Here we are not confronting raw evil: rather we are accompanying a remarkable young person as she grows into a spiritual fullness that each of us might envy. In general I am suspicious or at least cautious of such stories, as they degenerate too easily into a sentimental hagiography that prevents rather than encourages our own maturation. But there is a freshness and integrity about this story that makes it a good example by which to illustrate the idea of companionship in the search for the Kingdom. You may have experienced something of the inner loneliness that afflicts anyone who struggles seriously with the evil and suffering of the world – whether that struggle be physical or spiritual. The cry of dereliction from the cross is the ultimate expression of loneliness before evil. As your prayer for the Kingdom deepens and matures, so you will know moments of dereliction. They are not, it hardly needs emphasis, to be sought (nor, for that matter, is their absence to be mourned). They are likely to come, sought or shirked, and it is well to be ready for them. Stories of companionship can help. They are not to be seen, as 'Lives of the Saints' used to be, as in any sense whatever models on which we are to base our own lives or prayers or expectations. That is to deny our individuality and God's love for us as we are. Rather, see them in the same light that you would see another angler's account of his day's fishing; or another dinghy sailor's account of the day's race – something to be shared, enjoyed, entered into, learnt from, compared, savoured. Then, when the dereliction strikes, you can hang on to the certain knowledge that the sense of loneliness is, at one level at least, illusory. Others have been here before – as when Joe got his last Greenwell's Glory caught 15 feet up an alder or Mike had his dinghy capsize within a yard of the finishing line.

¶Read Cathy's story two or three times. We have here essentially two stories: one about costly identification; the other about losing life to find it. To use the first as a companionship story, let yourself *be with* Cathy in what she does, what she fears, what she suffers. Tell yourself the story in the first person plural, in the present tense. 'We have heard the Ngati Whatua are going to camp on the point to keep the developers out. We are going to join them. What will Mum and Dad think? Our friends? Never mind. We're going. . . . The police are arriving. . . . Wow, they look pretty tough. . . .'As you are going through this, you will have to work hard to recreate the story with you yourself alongside Cathy. You will be identifying with her. That's the first step.

The second, which you will manage only when you have successfully completed the first, is to identify both of you with the Maoris. Unlike Cathy, you know little about Maori customs or language. That does not matter. What does matter is the feeling of Cathy standing alongside the Maoris as they are harassed and then arrested, as they are examined, ques-

tioned, insulted, kept hanging about in the police station. Just
be there. The cultural gap seems unbridgeable. See Cathy
bridge it . . . not by artificial chumminess, but by a shared
commitment to justice. . . . Draw strength. . . . Give
strength. . . . Watch as a fourteen-year-old schoolgirl explores
solidarity with men twice, three times her age from an alien
race and culture . . . and give thanks that such solidarity is
possible. Inner loneliness is not finally overcome thereby, but
as we approach or leave that absolute aloneness in which we
confront evil, we may be sustained by the certainty that we
are not the first to make this difficult journey.

The second part of Cathy's story needs to be read as a kind
of inner analogue of the first. In the first Cathy is directly
withstanding – and seeking to win round – the forces of
oppression: in the second, this conflict is internalized and, in
the process, literally revolutionized. Now she has to face the
deep, dark secret places of her own psyche and find for herself
both the positive forces of her own identity and, therein, the
saving power of God in her own life.

¶Try following her in that journey; laying aside the borrowed
habits of a life that is not truly hers; stripping and being
stripped of all that is not genuine, integral, of God. It is a
process of exquisite pain. Are you able to share that – or at
least some of that? Can you detect the gradual emergence of
a new life, in a true resurrection, that draws its beauty and
its strength from the deepest springs of personal wholeness,
and dedicates it to holiness? . . .

This is the hard, hard road to God himself: few of us experience the death and resurrection which constitute it either as
quickly or as early as Cathy. Yet the discovery of the life of
God in us, at our deepest point of personal consciousness, is
inseparable from prayer for the Kingdom. For facing the
powers of destruction, distortion and diminishment in our
selves is an integral part of struggling for the Kingdom. To
pray for its establishment but shirk that encounter is as
unavailing as it is blasphemous.

Finally, we come to the story of Flora. There are many

ways of meditating this story: you may want to think of ways yourself. Here is one to start you off.

¶In the extract I have reproduced, there are four pieces of direct speech. Three are hostile, threatening. 'Go away: you are rebels.' 'Stop your work or you will be stockaded.' 'Why are you disturbing my workers and causing trouble?' Enter imaginatively into the scenes that generate those threats. Are you frightened? . . . Do you want to stop the work? . . . How do you feel about those who utter those threats? . . . How do you respond?

Now look at the other bit of direct speech. 'I am a person, like you. These are my rights that I am demanding.' How does it feel to assert your humanity? . . . What does its assertion say about how you feel about God? . . . What does the demand of your rights say about the nature of God? . . . Try to compare and contrast how you feel when you are being abused and threatened with how you feel when you are asserting your right to be human, and to be treated as a human. And reflect what the difference in those feelings says to us about the Kingdom.

If you have worked through these stories conscientiously, you will probably have been surprised by the vehemence of your emotional reaction. You will have released your feelings by entering imaginatively into situations of conflict, difficulty and transformation, where the values of the Kingdom are under pressure and yet poking out round the edges of reality. This is a theme to which we shall have to return in the next chapter.

To repeat a word of encouragement, do not be alarmed or self-critical if you have found these exercises hard. It is not unlike jogging – the first few times are horrible, but as your physique develops so it becomes easier. I hope you will want to repeat these exercises again and again; or, better, develop your own based on your own experience. It will take time – and hard work. It *will* get easier. . . . You may develop your own approach that is somewhat different to the one I shall be using in the next three chapters. As I have already said, and will say again, do not try to cut that off. The best tribute you can pay this book is to throw it out of the window – as long as your prayer for the Kingdom is alive.

5

Story in the Old Testament

It is time now to move from 'getting inside' stories that
raise for us questions of the Kingdom to stories that tell us
something of the nature of God's longing for the Kingdom.
Without going deep into biblical criticism, it is helpful to
remember that the stories that we shall be looking at in this
chapter vary a great deal in their form, their historical
veracity, their origins, their original purposes, and the audience for which they were designed. Nearly all of them came
from a deeply meditated apprehension of the nature and
purposes of God. They are not journalistic rapportage or
political propaganda: they are attempts to express truths that
the writer (or his community) has glimpsed about ultimate
reality. We are trying to recapture that glimpse, appropriate
for ourselves that perception of the imperceptible, rather than
bandy texts or build of purple passages a highway to ideological certitude. For if the essence of prayer for the Kingdom
is to stand naked before God and withstand the powers of
evil, it is as well to know what kind of God we stand before.

The seven meditations in this chapter are designed to help
us do just that. Taken together they bring us face to face with
a God who calls his people into a loving relationship that
enables them to be all that he made them to be, who pines
for that relationship to be honestly and wholeheartedly
entered into and enjoyed, and who finally hints that paradoxically only suffering and death will bring that relationship
alive in its fullness. When that relationship is fully alive,
human attitudes, perceptions, ways of dealing with each
other, of behaving towards each other are, by that very fact,
so transformed that the Kingdom of God is established. God
calls us to a relationship with him: the initiative is his. Our
response therefore determines the possibilities of the coming

of the Kingdom. What then is the nature of the call he makes to us?

Call and promise

> God spoke to Moses and said to him, 'I am Yahweh. To Abraham and Isaac and Jacob I appeared as El Shaddai; I did not make myself known to them by my name Yahweh. Also, I made my covenant with them to give them the land of Canaan, the land they lived in as strangers. And I have heard the groaning of the sons of Israel, enslaved by the Egyptians, and have remembered my covenant. Say this, then, to the sons of Israel, "I am Yahweh. I will free you of the burdens which the Egyptians lay on you. I will release you from slavery to them, and with my arm outstretched and my strokes of power I will deliver you. I will adopt you as my own people, and I will be your God. Then you shall know that it is I, Yahweh your God, who have freed you from the Egyptians' burdens. Then I will bring you to the land I swore that I would give to Abraham, and Isaac, and Jacob, and will give it to you for your own; I, Yahweh, will do this!" ' Moses told this to the sons of Israel, but they would not listen to him, so crushed was their spirit and so cruel their slavery.   (Exodus 6: 2–9)

Read this passage two or three times – slowly. Let it sink in.

Try now to make a great effort of imagination. Become one of the Israelites to whom Moses brings this extraordinary offer. For background, read Exodus 5: 6–18.

¶You are a brickmaker, constantly toiling in the heat to make your daily tally of bricks. You have to dig the clay out of deep pits. The sun shines full; the breeze cannot reach you; the atmosphere is stifling. The clay is hard . . . You mix the clay with water and then with chopped straw to bulk it out and make it lighter. You ram the mixture into moulds, carry them to one side of the pit and lay the moulded bricks in the sun. . . . Then back to dig more clay. . . . The work is arduous, the conditions foul, the discipline, enforced with whips, severe. You resent the fact that fellow-Israelites collude with

the Egyptian slave drivers to extract the day's output. . . .
What else do you feel? What do you feel about Yahweh, your
God? Where is he?

Now trouble is increased. Moses has been to Pharaoh to
ask for some time off for you to worship Yahweh. As a reprisal
for this rebellious act, Pharaoh has withdrawn the supply of
straw. Now you must find it for yourself. That means going
into the fields – and increasingly distant fields as the nearby
supplies are used up – to cut stubble, a slow, backbreaking
task. . . . Try it. . . . And then run back to the clay pit, shouted
at and abused by your fellow Israelites, the foremen. They
are desperate. They know that if you don't produce enough
bricks, they will be whipped – again. So they give you a hard
time. . . . Now how do you feel about Moses? And about
Yahweh? And about what Moses says Yahweh told him to
say to Pharaoh?

The next night Moses calls you, your family and all the
people together. He tells you that Yahweh has spoken to him
in prayer again. Yahweh has told Moses that he will deliver
you from this slavery; that he will return you to the land of
Canaan which you've heard older generations describe in
mouth-watering terms. Yahweh, the indescribably transcendent God (for that is the meaning of his name), will adopt
you as his people. What does that mean for you now? . . .
How would you discuss it with your spouse after the meeting
with Moses? What trust would you put in that promise? What
courage would you put behind that trust?

Spend as long as you need to with those last two questions.
They are basic. For the coming of the Kingdom is today what
it was for the Israelites in Egypt – essentially a matter of trust
and courage. When you have lived through those questions
as an Israelite; that is, when you have decided how far you
would be prepared to trust Yahweh's promise and what risks
you would take in living out that trust, put them to yourself
in your present situation. What is God's offer to his people
today – what form of deliverance? What does it mean to be
'adopted' by God? How far will we trust it? What risks will
we take?

Most people who do this meditation tell me they find two
things: first a great temptation to 'spiritualize' out of existence

God's offer to his people today (can it possibly be that he *really* offers a quality of relationship that defeats fear, greed, envy and egocentricity so that peace and harmony become actual?); and second, a shattering discovery of the paucity of their trust and their reluctance to take the most modest risk. 'I was miserable as an Israelite in the clay pit,' reported one robust nun, 'but no way would I risk so much as a day's stubble-supply to follow that man Moses. Any more nonsense, and Pharaoh would impound our clay shovels and double the brick tally . . . no way!'

If you share either of those reactions, perhaps appropriate prayer may be for trust to take God seriously; and the courage to live out that trust, so that it ceases to be assent to intellectual propositions and becomes a way of life.

Idols

The relationship into which Yahweh calls the Israelites is one of grace. Yahweh adopts the people and offers himself as their deliverer, their guarantor, their final hope of restoration to the full status of free human beings living in community with each other and with him. Out of the clay pit into an association of the wholly free, the Kingdom itself. But the relationship can only work if it is mutual. Lovers have to be wholly committed to each other if their love is to survive and grow until it is so consuming that it transforms their priorities, their perceptions of each other and of the rest of their world. In other words the process of transformation which is precisely the coming of the Kingdom can only occur if the relationship of love is kept intact and growing. That is why the Old Testament puts such great emphasis on the need for Israel to be faithful to the covenant and, more specifically, to avoid diverting to other gods the loving care which is the prerogative of Yahweh. Idolatry is, therefore, the central ethical/religious concern of much of the Old Testament. For it is idolatry that literally makes the coming of the Kingdom impossible.

Take great care what you do, therefore: since you saw no shape on that day at Horeb when Yahweh spoke to you from the midst of the fire, see that you do not act perversely, making yourselves a carved image in the shape of anything at all: whether it be in the likeness of man or of woman, or of any beast on the earth, or of any bird that flies in the heavens, or of any reptile that crawls on the ground, or of any fish in the waters under the earth. When you raise your eyes to heaven, when you see the sun, the moon, the stars, all the array of heaven, do not be tempted to worship them and serve them. Yahweh your God has allotted them to all the peoples under heaven, but as for you, Yahweh has taken you, and brought you out from the furnace of iron, from Egypt, to be a people all his own, as you still are today.   (Deuteronomy 4:15–20)

Read the piece over two or three times. 'Take great care what you do' is a kind of chorus in this part of Deuteronomy, but it is the 'therefore' that is significant. For it refers back to the Covenant: the avoidance of idolatry is mandatory because Yahweh has chosen these people 'to be a people all his own'. It is this link, between election and faithfulness, that this meditation is designed to help us internalize. It is in three parts.

¶Start with the text – and your imagination. Notice that the contrast is between the invisibility, the ineffability, of Yahweh and the visible presence, the clamant immediacy of the idols. It is *because* Yahweh is so transcendent (as well as so close) that the temptation arises to have an image that can be apprehended. Try to enter into that contrast. The Israelites, remember, are surrounded by peoples who have very apprehensible gods, or, at the very least, visible gods like the sun, moon or stars. But you, as an Israelite, have no such easy prop to your faith. You have to trust – and be faithful – to a lover you never see, never hear, never touch. . . . Do you long for a totem or an image? How comfortable to have a god you can contain! . . . Feel that distinction between a domesticated god and the wildness of unsculpted love that is Yahweh. . . .

The second part of this exercise takes a closer look at modern idols. Take one or more of the following encapsulations of our culture – a colour magazine or newspaper supplement; a major speech, manifesto or platform of a significant national politician; the expenditure plans of the national government or a major agency of government (metropolitan council, state, city administration). Read whatever you choose (the advertisements are usually more revealing than the text in the magazines and newspapers) as though you were an Israelite suddenly transferred to this culture. What does it tell you about the gods of this culture? What are they? What do influential people (big businessmen, journalists, politicians) evidently regard as most important?

Most people who do this exercise (and it is good to do it in small groups if that is possible) come back with a fairly predictable list – glamour, sex appeal, power, prestige, security, 'success' (measured in a great variety of ways), domination over others. It is revealing, however, to try to get behind these gods. How are they presented? On what motives do they play? How do they elicit a response? (A strange parallelism lies between the Baalim of the Old Testament, which were usually phallic representations of one kind or another and the disguised use of phallic symbols in modern advertising and product design.)

Masters of the spiritual life have always been aware how readily we Christians follow our Israelite forebears into the delicious groves of idol-worship. St Ignatius, for example, has a meditation in which the demons of Satan are sent to tempt us, God's people, into riches, from which we will learn to lust after honour. Then, almost inevitably, we will become proud, and thereby enrol under Satan's banner. It is no accident that Jesuits and all who derive benefit from the Ignatian exercises still use that simple allegory as a way of discerning in themselves the threats to faithfulness to a loving relationship with God.

The last part of this meditation, therefore, is the hardest. Again it is ideally undertaken in a group that has some common allegiance – members of the same community; of a church council; of a family – but it can be done effectively by an individual too.

¶Take any major decision you as a group have recently been required to make, perhaps on the allocation of resources or of time, or on priorities or objectives. Ask yourselves what ultimate values finally decided you in that decision . . .

It may help if I illustrate from a lightly disguised case. A religious order met to decide whether or not to continue to staff and control a secondary school in a large, problem-ridden and depressed British city. The head of the Order suggested that the meeting consider the matter under two heads: was the school meeting a need? Was it meeting it well? In the discussion, it was emphasized that the school had three times as many applications as it had places; that increased fees had not deterred applications; that a significant proportion of the city's notable citizens were old pupils; that a high proportion of students went on to major universities. . . . Satan's demons must have chuckled as they saw recruits flocking to the wrong banner.

You may find it helpful, therefore, to finish this exercise by praying for the insight to spot the idols that surround us all, and the strength of love to resist them. For, to repeat a point made at the beginning of this exercise, the process of transformation of values, attitudes, perceptions and priorities which the coming of the Kingdom requires *can* only come about through a deepening love-affair with God. Once we lust after the values of the colour magazines or the politicians, we abandon the hope of the Kingdom. Yet how deep those false values and the idolatry they represent go in us all.

The law of living lovingly

If the central thrust of ethico-religious teaching of the Old Testament is the maintenance of the Covenant relationship and the implied avoidance of idolatry, its implication is that the economic, social and political life of the people of Israel must reflect the loving generosity of Yahweh's action in choosing Israel and acting lovingly in its history. This call to loving kindness in personal and social relations came to be embodied in the Torah, the Law. For modern Western peoples, the whole notion of 'law' has a chill, authoritarian ring. It is rational, male, concerned with rights. For Israel the law was quite different. It was celebration – celebration of God's love for them and their call to love each other. No wonder the Psalmist could exult in the law: 'Meditating all day on your Law, how I have come to love it . . . Sweeter than honey to my mouth' (Psalm 119:97, 103). It is hard to see a barrister or an attorney saying that as he reads the latest law report.

But for the Israelite, at its best the law was a working out of what loving kindness means in everyday relationships.

'You must not pervert justice in dealing with a stranger or an orphan, nor take a widow's garment in pledge. Remember that you were a slave in Egypt and that Yahweh your God redeemed you from there. That is why I lay this charge on you.

'When reaping the harvest in your field, if you have overlooked a sheaf in that field, do not go back for it. Leave it for the stranger, the orphan and the widow, so that Yahweh your God may bless you in all your undertakings.

'When you beat your olive trees you must not go over the branches twice. Let anything left be for the stranger, the orphan and the widow.

'When you harvest your vineyard you must not pick it over a second time. Let anything left be for the stranger, the orphan and the widow.

'Remember that you were a slave in the land of Egypt. That is why I lay this charge on you. (Deuteronomy 24:17–22)

Read that passage two or three more times – slowly. Remember that the key thing about the widow, the orphan and the stranger is that they had no claim to land of their own. They were therefore symbols of those who could expect nothing as of right: exactly parallel with the legal, ethical and religious condition of Israel with respect to Yahweh. Israel as a people had to depend on Yahweh's love; nothing more. They had no *claim* on it. The widow, the orphan and the stranger had no *claim* on society. As Yahweh had redeemed Israel, so now the people must celebrate that liberation by showing the same loving generosity to those who had no claim on them.

It is this ethic that we need to let come alive in us. It is the ethic that I shall call, after Jean Vanier, the ethic of gratuity. That is a word that many people find difficult. 'To people in my station in life', said a wealthy but well-meaning friend, 'gratuity is what you give the boot boy.' Perhaps, but in its original, deeper meaning gratuity was the virtue of overwhelming love expressing itself in almost excessive generosity, A Parsee friend of mine had a grandmother who was very, very rich. Living in Karachi in the last years of the last century, she was inevitably surrounded by poor people who hoped for the odd crumbs that might fall from her table. A deeply religious woman, she was so generous that her family easily foresaw the early disappearance of the family fortune. They stopped her carrying money so she couldn't give it away. They ensured that no poor person was allowed to enter the house so she wouldn't give away the precious furniture and priceless ornaments. They even locked her cupboards so she could not give away her own clothes. One day a toothless old woman somehow managed to wheedle her way into the drawing room and confronted the lady of the house. 'A sari, a sari,' she cried, 'Just an old sari. This rag is all I have.' 'I cannot give you a sari,' the lady of the house explained, 'for they have locked all the cupboards. But if you don't mind washing this . . . ,' and she took off the richly decorated silk sari she was wearing and presented it to the old woman. She thus offended her family as much by appearing undressed before a stranger as by continuing her profligate generosity. . . . Such is gratuity, and while I am aware of the peculiar ring of the word, perhaps that story will restore enough of its true meaning to permit me to use it hereafter.

To bring about the notion of gratuity – for it is an ethic that applies to communities and nations as well as individuals – here is an exercise you might like to try with the passage from Deuteronomy in mind.

¶Imagine you are a small farmer, growing corn. Yours is a family farm, just large enough to keep you and your two sons. It is a hard life and, as agricultural policy and technology increasingly favour the larger farmer, it is getting harder. Just before harvest, there is a serious disaster in another part of the country, and an aid agency asks all farmers to give one

61

ton of corn in five to help feed those at risk. You have to decide how you will respond to that request.

What would enable you to respond joyfully and cheerfully? A law, passed by government, demanding an extra tax of 20 per cent of your production? A direct request from the people concerned? Television pictures of starving children? . . . Or the heart-knowledge of being loved so freely and generously that a joyful response is the only one available to you?

Law, direct requests, television pictures may all produce a response – but it will be a reluctant, half-hearted or guilt-ridden response. That is far removed from the gratuity of the Covenant – and from the love ethic of the Kingdom. That ethic, of course, does not wait for the declaration of a state of emergency to raise fundamental questions about economic morality.

Consider the contrast between the corn farmer who gives lovingly because he is loved; and the profit-maximizing farmer who abuses his land, pays the barest minimum to his labour (especially if they are illegal immigrants), and strips his fields of the last cob of corn. One lives by gratuity; the other lives for money.

This living by gratuity is so fundamental to the Kingdom and so remote from Western styles of financial thinking, that the next part of this exercise focuses upon it.

¶Watch Christ coming as a gypsy or a 'traveller' or an illegal immigrant to each of the farmers in the last paragraph. He wants a meal, somewhere to sleep, perhaps a couple of days' casual labour. Dusty and tired, dishevelled, unshaven, he knocks on the door of the profit-maximizing farmer . . .

Watch what happens. . . . What does Christ say? . . . What does the farmer say? . . . How does Christ feel . . . when he remembers the Cross? . . . Watch him go to the door of the farmer who has allowed himself to be loved into living by gratuity. . . . What is the farmer's response? . . . Watch them sit down together to eat. . . . How does it feel in that kitchen?

In the light of what you have experienced of this paradigm shift, from egocentricity to gratuity, reflect upon the story of the Franciscan community in El Salvador in chapter 4. Take them as symbols of all those who have lived that shift. Thank

God for them and for what they represent. And pray for grace to make that shift. For here we depart abruptly from the world of Deuteronomy. We leave law and enter the realm of grace. Gratuity comes not so much from law as from the lived experience of being loved. That is grace. We pray, therefore, that we may become so conscious of the love of God for us that grace can become a reality in our lives – and through that grace we can make that critical leap from self-centredness to the loving generosity of gratuity.

There is a danger that we allow our meditation on this theme, and the prayer that springs naturally from that meditation, to become over-individualistic. Of course, we have to accept responsibility for our own responses, our own apprehension of a love so profound that it both enables and demands a response. But the Law of the Old Testament was not only an individual's moral code: it defined a spirit in which whole communities could live – and live more fully.

To 'get a feel' of this, it might be helpful to repeat the core of this exercise, substituting nations for farmers. What would enable a nation to respond joyfully and generously to the needs of 600 million people without the means of a basic subsistence? We look to United Nations norms, political leadership, grass roots pressure, self-interest. That they can do something is not in question. That they can do rather little has been amply demonstrated. Dare we pray for the paradigm shift from self-interest to gratuity, from half-heartedness to loving generosity? We can only pray meaningfully in such terms in the context of a world made aware of how much God loves it. For that is the basis of the shift in paradigm. To that extent there can be no logical or spiritual division between prayer for justice and prayer for mission. The Kingdom comprehends both. If we are to pray for a world that conducts its affairs in a spirit of loving gentleness, we are committed to prayer for a world that knows, in the heart and in the soul rather than in the mind, how much it is cherished.

The threat from institutions

That this inner consciousness of the love of God has to be a lived reality rather than an intellectual proposition is central to the Kingdom. For the natural human pressures are to cut oneself off from the full grandeur of God's love and seek to contain it, control it, tame it, make it predictable and manageable. Most people are deeply frightened of unconditional love and its power to expand the freedom of the loved one. They therefore want to institutionalize it, regulate it, surround it with restrictions, conventions – anything to make it safe.

That is the tragic paradox. Love that is offered to make people free is so overpowering that it is quickly encased, and thereby robs people of the very freedom it was destined to secure.

This encasement, this institutionalization takes many forms. These are hinted at in the passage below: *ritualization* of a relationship so that it ceases to live; *taking the relationship for granted* so that we cease to try to make it alive; the *commercialization* of the relationship so that its life, already rendered false, can be controlled by cash. Transformation of attitudes or the paradigm shift to gratuity is thus safely put out of court. Paradox indeed: a world that shows every need of transformation neuters the one source of power that would make that transformation possible.

'Come, let us return to Yahweh.
He has torn us to pieces, but he will heal us;
he has struck us down, but he will bandage our wounds;
after a day or two he will bring us back to life,
on the third day he will raise us
and we shall live in his presence.
Let us set ourselves to know Yahweh;
that he will come is as certain as the dawn
his judgement will rise like the light,
he will come to us as showers come,
like spring rains watering the earth.'
What am I to do with you, Ephraim?
What am I to do with you, Judah?
This love of yours is like a morning cloud,

like the dew that quickly disappears.
This is why I have torn them to pieces by the prophets,
why I slaughtered them with the words from my mouth,
since what I want is love, not sacrifice;
knowledge of God, not holocausts.   (Hosea 6:1–6)

Read the passage two or three times more. Do you hear the
ironic tone of the second half? Yahweh is mocking the half-
heartedness of Israel. They assume that he will soon restore
their fortunes. No need to worry; no need to really put their
backs into the relationship. Notice the ironic contrast between
Israel seeing Yahweh's love as showers or spring rains; and
Yahweh dismissing Israel's love as dew that soon dries up.
Israel has, as it were, become cut off from the deep spiritual
roots of the Covenant. Now the Covenant relationship is form,
not content; it is style, not substance; it is platitude, not
vibrant hope.

It can therefore be both formalized and manipulated.
Corruption of worship and the sacrificial system provided the
means. Instead of being ways by which trust and love could
be expressed and nourished, they became means by which
God could be conned – or bought. What was meant to be
a passionate love affair, pregnant with the possibilities of
transformation, became a process of mechanical satisfaction.

¶It might be a good idea to dwell on the anguish of that
repeated cry, 'What am I to do with you . . . ?' It resonates
with memories of loving parents in near despair with
wayward, selfish children who refuse every opportunity to
grow into a fuller realization of their potential.

It is probable that you have some such memory, perhaps
as a parent or a sympathetic observer of a family caught in
the agony of suspended development. Enter into the frustrated
expectation of love: allow yourself to feel the pain of unreal-
ized potential in one you love deeply. 'If only . . .'

There is moreover rejection here. The potential that is unreal-
ized is not only potential to grow into a greater maturity; it
is potential to grow into a deeper love of you. The reluctance,
perhaps the final incapacity, to let go of false securities and
make that commitment is one of the gravest wounds we can

ever inflict on each other. There is, then, an almost intolerable pain in those seven words.

¶Move on now to the penultimate line. 'What I want is love.' What could be more explicit, more vulnerable? The anguish of the rejected lover or the emotionally deprived child is unsustainable. Nothing will substitute for the love he craves. All pretence has gone. And with it the protection of dignity. 'What I want . . .' But, continues Yahweh two lines later, 'they have proved unfaithful.' The dereliction is complete.

And Israel does not even understand what she is doing. The mockery of the first half of the passage thus has a deeper tone of anguish. Israel says, 'Let us set ourselves to know Yahweh,' without any comprehension of either the costliness or the glory of that resolve. They paddle in the shallows without realizing the possibilities of the deeps. Like an accomplished flirt, they play at a relationship they don't mean, and never give a thought to the damage they do to the victim of their flirtation.

The anger, the hurt, the frustration, the sense of betrayal cannot be contained. 'I have torn them to pieces . . . I have slaughtered them . . .'

What has this to do with the Kingdom? That is made explicit by Jesus' quotation of the last lines of this passage (Matthew 9:13). The context is crucial. In the arrangement of Matthew's Gospel, the gratuity of the Kingdom is *taught*, preached in the Sermon on the Mount (chapters 5 to 7). That gratuity is then *lived* by the performance of ten miracles, all of them healing – or symbols of healing like the calming of the storm (chapters 8 and 9). Two-thirds of the way through this part of the Gospel, the opposition raises its head. The Pharisees complain that Jesus is in technical breach of the laws of purity because he eats with tax collectors and sinners.

They thus reveal that they have not begun to understand what the Kingdom is about. Exactly like Israel in Hosea's day, they want to control it, keep it safely in a box to be opened only by the right people at the right time. Jesus' reply is heavy with irony, and he reminds them of the prophetic tradition that has insisted on the radically transformative possibilities of the love of God. It cannot be contained within

66

a book of rules, and it cannot be limited to those who live by a book of rules. For they are proof against transformation.

The second part of this exercise may help root the openness of the love of God in the contemporary world, and underline the centrality of that openness to the process of transform-ation. We must return to the story of Cathy, and read it as a parable of the de-institutionalization of God's transforming love. Brought up in a 'good', 'religious' home, with loving Christian parents, she senses that there is something phoney or ersatz about her own spiritual values. She has to break out of the formalized, conventional constraints that can give her everything but nothing, the menu but not the meal. Only when she has struggled free of all that mediates, filters, distorts and sets bounds on the love of God can she be remade into a person in whom the Kingdom is clearly coming.

¶I want you to meditate on that costly, potentially destructive, always dangerous period when she has left home and gone in search of her own encounter with God's love. But don't live out that adventure through Cathy: look for it in your own experience. . . . And then in the experience of your congre-gation, your parish . . . and finally in the Church as a whole.

There is no need to be surprised or dismayed if you have difficulty finding much material on which to work. Ask your-self then at which end of the journey you find yourself: have you completed it so that God does not need to groan, 'What am I to do with you . . .'? Or has it not yet begun so that we can hardly hear him saying it?

These are such huge questions that it is impertinent to guide you towards specific prayer. It may be important, however, to end by dwelling on the fact that 'What I want is love . . .' may be a deliberate pun. While the parallelism suggests that the primary meaning is love of God, as we have so far understood it, a secondary meaning is, as other translations have it, mercy or loving kindness. In other words, the demand for radical love of God is indistinguishable from radical love of those who have no claim on us. So prayer comes to focus on that vortex: where freedom to give and receive the abundance of God's love spills over into, comprehends, includes, becomes the essence of the splendour of love of the vulnerable and the dispossessed.

'What I want is love'

So far we have seen that the love affair between Yahweh and Israel was constantly in jeopardy from idolatry and institutionalization. (We might have explored the way in which the former includes the latter: how religious people worship institutions, procedures and formalities.) God's love for his people was constantly trying to break through, and as constantly being rebuffed. It was rebuffed at two levels: by the way in which Israel chased foreign gods (a direct rebuff) and by the way in which the people of Israel ignored the laws of gratuity in their dealings with their own poor and defenceless (an indirect rebuff). Both forms of rejection were cause and effect of the institutionalization of a relationship. A mechanical routine made a tumultuous love easily liveable with. What should have been a real marriage had been reduced to a comfortable living arrangement. The energy of love that could have transformed Israel into a community that made evident the coming of the Kingdom had been turned off at its source.

That is the ethical agony of the Old Testament. It is the agony of opportunities thrown away; of possibility made impossible. No wonder Yahweh, as seen through an earlier religious consciousness, becomes angry, disenchanted and outraged. Naturally the centre of that anger is the sense of rejection, of love spurned. Its reflection, however, is anger that the values of the Kingdom are inevitably beyond the capacity of the people of Israel – beyond their capacity to conceive as well as to achieve. The poor and the ordinary people, as opposed to the rich, the educated and the powerful, are therefore oppressed in a direct reversal of what the Kingdom stands for.

To crown the irony, the righteous are puzzled by God's inaction on behalf of the poor. Like fishermen who pray for a catch but fail to bait the hook, they expect Yahweh to deliver the poor within a society that refuses to honour the Covenant. In an ethical backward somersault, they look for

Yahweh to ignore his offer to the whole people of God; and then expect him to tinker with the mechanics when things go wrong.

By contrast with the historians of the Moses tradition and with the prophets, here is a piece by a relatively late philosopher-poet. It comes, of course, in the context of the discussion between Job and his comforters, at the point where Job reflects on the transcendence, even the distance, of God and the resulting triumph of evil. Here then is a typical inversion of the reality of Covenant love. Israel turns her back on God and then says she cannot see him. Social breakdown is the inevitable result.

> Why has not Shaddai his own store of times, and why do his faithful never see his Days?
> The wicked move boundary-marks away, they carry off flock and shepherd.
> Some drive away the orphan's donkey, and take the widow's ox for a security.
> Beggars, now, avoid the roads, and all the poor of the land must go into hiding.
> Like wild donkeys in the desert, they go out, driven by the hunger of their children, to seek food on the barren steppes.
> They must do the harvesting in the scoundrel's field, they must do the picking in the vineyards of the wicked.
> They go about naked, lacking clothes, and starving while they carry the sheaves.
> They have no stones for pressing oil, they tread the winepresses, yet they are parched with thirst.
> They spend the night naked, lacking clothes, with no covering against the cold.
> Mountain rainstorms cut them through, shelterless, they hug the rocks.
> Fatherless children are robbed of their lands, and poor men have their cloaks seized as security.
> From the towns come the groans of the dying and the gasp of wounded men crying for help. Yet God remains deaf to their appeal!

(Job 24:1–12)

I can never read this passage without a sickening sense of *déjà-vu*. For every verse finds its exact equivalent in many parts of the world. 'The wicked move boundary-marks . . .' We have seen that already in New Zealand. It happens constantly in Brazil where large corporations buy the 'right' to settle huge tracts of land already occupied by poor peasants who are then forced, often after some have been killed, to move out. 'They carry off flock and shepherd . . .' Ask the Navajo in New Mexico about that. 'Beggars now avoid the roads and all the poor of the land must go into hiding.' Immediately Guatemala and El Salvador come into mind. In neither country is it safe to be seen by the military authorities if you happen to be poor.

It would be good if you could carry on, looking for that kind of parallel. You will find many for each verse in the passage. Some will strike you immediately. Others can sit quietly at the back of your mind until you stumble, as you certainly will, across a story or a reference that matches it.

The crunch comes with the final line. 'God remains deaf to their appeal.' So says Job – or the philosopher poet who wrote Job. As he makes clear in the dénouement, that is not his final position. 'I retract all I have said and in dust and ashes I repent' (Job 42:6). Our central meditative position is, of course, to start from the very opposite view. God hears and grieves for the oppressed and the defenceless. His reaction is to go on offering Israel his love, because only that will transform them into a community that will not permit the injustices described in the passage. He offers that love – and has it thrown back in his face.

We need, then, to hold those two perspectives in tension: God offering the possibility of transforming love and the consequences of its rejection. By allowing ourselves to feel the pain and horror of the oppressed, we can begin to share the suffering of Yahweh as he sees his people reject him. For he is there in the misery of the oppressed: so far from 'remaining deaf', he enters into that suffering and longs for it to end. 'What I want is love . . . ,' because that love will bring an end to the suffering of his people.

¶Can we, then, go through the list of parallels we have made, and share the suffering with God? Offer it to him, allowing it to hurt us as we do so . . . Can we share his longing for his people to respond to the love he offers them?

We are now near the heart of prayer for the Kingdom. For we are standing before God sharing his sharing in the agony of the world. But it is not a hopeless or depressing exchange of misery. For there at the heart of God we see the creative power that can break through that agony, that longs to break through. In quiet and humility, we seek to ally ourselves with that power. . . .

At this point words become unhelpful. . . . You might like to end the exercise by thanking God for all those who in their daily lives bring him the agony of the world. For the most part they are his poor and under-educated; the uninfluential and unimportant. Because they know the cost of the Kingdom's delay, they offer him a longing that matches his own. Thank God for them – and for the longing they share with him.

Source of security

God longs for his people to be free. In a sense that is both historically actual and simultaneously symbolic; he frees them from Egypt, but then sees them enslave themselves in their own pride and egocentricity. He waits for them to return to the Covenant relationship in which, he keeps assuring them, he 'will be their God'. This is a guarantee of their prosperity, their security, their ultimate victory over all that threatens them from within and without. One aspect of their rejection of his love is the way that Isreael's politicians refuse to accept this assurance. Rather than trust him to be faithful to the Covenant which he initiated, they constantly search for more tangible sources of security – like bits of paper signed by the Assyrians or the Egyptians. Like the lover taking out a breach-of-contract insurance while her suitor is in her arms, Israel looks for military security and economic success to her traditional enemies, while ignoring the promise of her original liberator.

Woe to those rebellious sons! – it is Yahweh who speaks.

They carry out plans that are not mine and make alliances
not inspired by me, and so add sin to sin.

They have left for Egypt, without consulting me, to take
refuge in Pharaoh's protection, to shelter in Egypt's
shadow.

Pharaoh's protection will be your shame, the shelter of
Egypt's shadow your confounding.

For his ministers have gone to Zoan, his ambassadors have
already reached Hanes.

All are carrying gifts, to a nation that will be of no use to
them, that will bring them neither aid, nor help, nothing
but shame and disgrace.

For thus says the Lord Yahweh, the Holy One of Israel:
Your salvation lay in conversion and tranquillity, your
strength, in complete trust; and you would have none of
it.   (Isaiah 30:1–5, 15)

Judah was in trouble, threatened by Sennacherib, King of
Assyria in 702 B.C. Hezekiah, King of Judah, first tried to
buy him off by stripping the silver and gold plating from the
Temple, and then sought to make a treaty with 'that broken
reed, Egypt' (as Sennacherib's army commander described
it). Despite assurances of Yahweh's protection delivered
through Isaiah (2 Kings 19:6–7), Hezekiah preferred to rely
on Egypt for 'Chariots and horsemen', perhaps alarmed by
rumours (or propaganda) that it was Yahweh himself who
had sent Assyria against Judah. 'Yahweh himself said to me:
"March against this country and lay it waste"' (2 Kings
18:25).

But the prophet is faithful to the basic religious conviction
of the deepest springs of Jewish consciousness: 'Your salvation
lay in conversion and tranquillity; your strength in complete
trust.' But, he continues, 'you would have none of it'. Typical.
Judah simply will not accept that Yahweh will be true to his
Covenant promise. In a subtle mutation of idolatry, Judah
prefers to trust in the notoriously fickle and ineffectual Egyptians rather than in Yahweh's loving providence.

¶To bring this alive, I want you to imagine that you and any
group with which you are associated (your family, your
church council, your community) are in Hezekiah's court at

the time this argument is going on. There is a group of courtiers who want to do a deal with the Egyptians at almost any price. There is a smaller group round Isaiah, whom many regard as a religious maverick who think that all will be well providing you all trust Yahweh. And there is a big group in the middle who do not know what to do. Unfortunately the enemy seems to know of your divisions – and their spokesman is equally dismissive of both options. What is clear is that the Assyrians *are* very strong. Sennacherib has a formidable reputation and if it comes to a straight fight, there can be little doubt that, without substantial reinforcements, you will be defeated. The resulting carnage will be too terrible to bear contemplation.

What do you do?

The temptation is to say, 'Trust Yahweh,' because that is the 'right' answer. But if we say that too soon or too glibly, either our imagination or our honesty is . . . well, in need of further examination. I suspect this comes home to us when we translate this scenario into modern terms.

Imagine you are a member of the Cabinet. There is a proposal to strike a deal with the Russians for the elimination of all strategic missiles. Unfortunately, there is some question about the reliability of the verification procedures. It could just be that the Russians will *pretend* to destroy all their missiles but keep some hidden or at sea, thus securing a substantial military advantage. In the Cabinet is one oddball, suffering a bad attack of religious mania, who seems to think that all you need to do is to trust in God and try to live a godly life and the difficult technical questions of verifiability will be irrelevant. Against him is a large group of influential ministers who think it highly irresponsible (a word of which they seem peculiarly fond) to sign any treaty with the Russians until it has been established without a shadow of doubt that they will perform to the letter. . . . On whose side do you speak?

(In a way this 'translation' is unfair. NATO is not God's elected people in the way that Judah was invited to believe she was. But the Church is; and in however small a minority in NATO countries, the Church is called to the same quality of trust and obedience.)

The question this fantasy poses is familiar but fundamental. Is the love of God for his people to be trusted – or not? Is security to be found in weapons, alliances and all the sophisticated acts of diplomacy and 'defence' – or in simple trust in a God who yearns for his people's love?

So far we have posed the question in the same terms as they are posed in the Old Testament – those of military security. That is right and proper. Too easily we dilute the biblical insistence that Yahweh is the lord of history: that he works his purposes out in the political events of the day if he is given the elbow room to do so by the faith of his people. But security is not only a military concept. Many of the forces that embody values and perceptions that militate against the Kingdom stem from the desire for economic security, whether individual, class or national. Much of the international economic system, with its inbuilt bias in favour of the rich and the powerful, stems less from a conscious wish to exploit the poor of the world than a semi-conscious anxiety to protect the interests of the affluent. Those who keep it in place 'take refuge' in 'the protection' of restrictive trading arrangements (interestingly often labelled 'protection'), differential pricing mechanisms and unequal access to market opportunities, fearing that the laws of gratuity will destroy them. Refusing to believe that Yahweh wishes only their highest good, we not only refuse to trust him; but also, in withholding that trust, commit ourselves to an economic system that can only add to the oppression of the poor.

Perhaps a fitting way to conclude this exercise is to meditate briefly on an oracle that follows shortly after the one quoted above. (While it is found only a few verses later in the text, at Isaiah 30:19–26, it is almost certainly much later in historical context. Probably written during the exile, it is not an oracle of the Isaiah known to Hezekiah. It may have been offered by a prophet who saw himself as standing in the tradition of Isaiah.) It is a promise of restoration, of prosperity, of Yahweh's love for his people being worked out in practice. 'Whether you turn to right or left', writes the prophet in a graphic representation of the hesitation of the people of God, 'your ears will hear these words behind you: "This is the way. Follow it." You will regard your silvered idols and gilded images as unclean. You will throw them away like the polluted things they are, shouting after them, "Good riddance!" ' (Isaiah 30:21–3).

¶That is something to pray for, the day when we can all throw away our protections – whether they be bombs, restrictive trading agreements or inappropriate or harmful technologies – with the joyous relief that says, 'Good riddance'. The key to that day comes in a linking couplet at verse 18:

> Yahweh is waiting to be gracious to you,
> to rise and take pity on you,
> for Yahweh is a just God;
> happy are all who hope in him.

'Waiting to be gracious . . .' That picture of Yahweh waiting to show us his love is entirely consistent with the longing we have already encountered. It is a longing that is frustrated until we hope or trust in him. . . . Dwell, then, in the contrast and yet complementarity between more and more of his people wanting to say 'Good riddance' to devices that are inherently evil: and God waiting to be gracious. . . . Pray that he will not have to wait much longer.

Suffering

An impasse is reached. Yahweh waits to be gracious in response to his people's loving trustfulness. Seduced by false gods, his people cut themselves off from the transforming energy that will alone deliver them from their unfaithfulness. The trauma of defeat and deportation has very limited effect: certainly the promise of restoration does little to rekindle the passionate love that the Covenant relationship is supposed to be.

How can it be rekindled? The vision of the Suffering Servant in Isaiah (again, not Hezekiah's Isaiah: the Suffering Servant songs were written during the exile) begins to hint, in hauntingly beautiful but always ambiguous outline, where the answer might lie.

The four songs of the Suffering Servant are surrounded by academic controversy. Do they refer to Israel? Do they foretell an individual redeemer? What is his relationship, if any, to the monarchy? . . . and so on. In a way, the ambiguity is the point. The Songs are invitations to faith, to trust. They are not legally enforceable guarantees signed in triplicate. Nor are they a do-it-yourself handbook on 'How to Transcend the Human Condition'. They have all the subtlety and suggestiveness of good poetry and, as poetry, stimulate the imagination and intuition. No certainties, then; only hints.

The strongest hint is that the key to the impasse is to be found in suffering freely accepted by the Servant on behalf of those who cannot accept or respond to Covenant love. By completely identifying himself with the pain and anguish of the people, maybe he can enable them to open themselves to the recreative possibilities of a quality of love they cannot at present apprehend.

Like a sapling he grew up in front of us,
like a root in arid ground.
Without beauty, without majesty (we saw him),
no looks to attract our eyes;
a thing despised and rejected by men,
a man of sorrows and familiar with suffering,
a man to make people screen their faces;
he was despised and we took no account of him.
And yet ours were the sufferings he bore,
ours the sorrows he carried.
But we, we thought of him as someone punished,
struck by God, and brought low.
Yet he was pierced through for our faults,
crushed for our sins.
On him lies a punishment that brings us peace,
and through his wounds we are healed.
We had all gone astray like sheep,
each taking his own way,
and Yahweh burdened him
with the sins of all of us.
Harshly dealt with, he bore it humbly,
he never opened his mouth,
like a lamb that is led to the slaughter-house,
like a sheep that is dumb before its shearers
never opening its mouth.

(Isaiah 53:2–7)

It is hard to read this passage without immediately relating it to Jesus. We will come to that. For the moment, our meditation can go in quite a different direction. The poem suggests that suffering accepted on behalf of others can 'bring peace', can 'heal', even to those who have 'taken their own way'. Here then is a ringing declaration of the power of love expressed in suffering to change the values and perceptions of even the most purblind.

To put it another way, the process of the Kingdom's establishment is hastened by every act of redemptive love that is such a reflection of the Covenant love of Yahweh that wretched men and women are turned in their tracks and enabled to come alive.

¶Perhaps you could think of any such redemptive love you have seen in action. It may be on a modest scale; that is wholly immaterial. The touchstone is a quality of love that inevitably entails costly sacrifice to enable others to grow out of their egocentricity.

My own experience is that, perhaps surprisingly, the world is full of people who offer such love: indeed we met a number of them in the last chapter. Perhaps the best example is the Franciscans in El Salvador. There we see a costly sacrifice made in love that has quite literally transformed the lives of the many refugees, some soldiers, and even a few hard-bitten journalists and television crews.

If you find then, that you cannot now call to mind anyone who seems to exemplify this vocation, reflect on the Franciscans (or any of the other stories in chapter 4) in the light of the Suffering Servant.

Prayer for the Kingdom involves us in psychic and spiritual identification with the Suffering Servants of our generation. For they can and do release an energy of transformation that is unstoppable. By allowing us to glimpse in their lives a quality of love that has radically changed them, they put us in touch with the power of the Kingdom. How we react to it is then our judgement on ourselves. If we walk away from it, we enslave ourselves in a world that will never know the Kingdom. If we open ourselves to it, identify ourselves with it . . . what then?

That is the second part of this exercise. And it is hard, a stumbling block. For the record surely is – from Isaiah to the Gospels to the Epistles and throughout the life of the Church – that if we identify with the redemptive suffering love of the Kingdom, we run a substantial risk that we shall find ourselves called to live it. That is not something we should officiously seek or lay upon ourselves, like over-eager school children anxious to demonstrate how grown-up they are by volunteering for difficult chores. That can only lead to pseudo-love and spiritual pride of the most destructive variety.

Rather, I take it as a law of spiritual growth that as we are enabled to enter into the depth of love that the Songs of the Suffering Servant portray, we are gently drawn (*never* driven: if it feels like being driven, it is false – ignore it) to a situation in life where we can choose to accept redemptive suffering for ourselves.

¶To conclude this exercise, then, we can rest quietly in inner silence, with the contemplation of the poem and our identification with its present analogues settling gently at the back of our minds, and test our vocation to live that kind of love. . . .

Two footnotes: Despite my use of the phrase 'law of spiritual growth', God is not bound by laws. The vocation we are considering is a gift. God gives it to some and not to others. There is no need for despair or a sense of failure if he withholds it.

Second, spiritual growth is just that – growth. Nearly all natural growth is slow, almost imperceptible. It is well, then, to keep returning to this exercise. Allow it to become part of your regular prayer life.

In much current thinking about praying for the Kingdom it is fashionable to use the Old Testament, if at all, as a quarry for prophetic denunciations against the rich (of which there is certainly no shortage) or for threats of imminent disaster in judgement of oppression (of which there are more). That is not only to neglect the richness of the Old Testament, it is to risk seriously abusing the tradition. Like a reformed alcoholic sipping gin under the assumption that it is water, we under-estimate the power of the central religious truths to which Jesus and the early Church were heirs.

In the journey we have made in search of an approach to the Kingdom rooted in the religious consciousness of the Old Testament we have found that Covenant love is central. It is a passionate affair of the heart, the energy of which can transform human relationships and institutions; and make them the stuff of the Kingdom. Yahweh constantly offers that love and the recreative energy that comes from it – 'What I want is love . . .' – but it is spurned in favour of false gods and false friends. The result is that human and social relation-ships, deprived of the energy required to set them free from the selfishnesses that distort them, retain all the familiarly dreary characteristics of oppression, injustice and self-regard. Despite the shock of exile, Israel shows little readiness to enter afresh into the full ardour of the love affair of the Covenant. The stage is then set for a new initiative, a further attempt to woo the loveless, so cosily protected by their insti-tutions and pseudo-religious paraphernalia, back into a reck-less love. But this time Yahweh will himself, so the poem of the Servant hints, share the pain of the victims of his people. Love that shares the deepest suffering of humanity is to be offered in the hope that it will achieve what Covenant love has failed to do – transform the deepest wells of human action. The springs of deliverance will be offered in unconditional vulnerability.

6

The Kingdom offered

The Gospels proclaim the same message as the Old Testament. God loves and longs for his people, and when they can respond to that love they will be able to live the new life of peace, justice and harmony. The story of Jesus Christ is the story of a fresh appeal to God's people made in the flesh of one person. The Kingdom, the era of God's uncontested rule, is described and enacted. There it is for all who wish to see, to touch. It proves too much. The people can neither comprehend nor apprehend it. So they reject it. Not surprisingly they are led, even goaded, into that decision by the leaders of institutional religion, who see in the gratuity of the Kingdom too stark a challenge to their own power and security.

So much is closely parallel to the Old Testament story we followed in the last chapter. Whereas that finishes with a foretaste of redemptive suffering, this story, the New Testament, not only presents that redemptive suffering as a historical fact but also makes it the fulcrum of yet another offer of love and acceptance to the people – any people who will respond wholeheartedly to it. The rejection of the Kingdom at Golgotha does not end the creative possibilities of the new life of the Kingdom: they are re-presented in the resurrection and Pentecost. And, crucially, they are given a new dynamic in the Person of the Holy Spirit.

This chapter and the next, then, contain eleven meditative exercises that follow that story, based on the Gospels. While their form, structure and content naturally vary, their cumulative effect is to enable us to stand on the side of the poor and the frightened before a God who is in love with them. These exercises are in no sense exclusive or definitive. If your prayer takes off after reading one of the Bible passages below, let it soar. You will pray the Kingdom more authentically and more lovingly that way than by slavishly following the mechanics of the exercise. God is in love with you, not with this book.

The Kingdom offered

He went on to speak to them in parables, 'A man planted a vineyard; he fenced it round, dug out a trough for the winepress and built a tower; then he leased it to tenants and went abroad. When the time came, he sent a servant to the tenants to collect from them his share of the produce from the vineyard. But they seized the man, thrashed him and sent him away empty-handed. Next he sent another servant to them; him they beat about the head and treated shamefully. And he sent another and him they killed; then a number of others; and they thrashed some and killed the rest. He had still someone left: his beloved son. He sent him to them last of all. "They will respect my son," he said. But those tenants said to each other, "This is the heir. Come on, let us kill him, and the inheritance will be ours." So they seized him and killed him and threw him out of the vineyard. Now what will the owner of the vineyard do? He will come and make an end of the tenants and give the vineyard to others. Have you not read this text of scripture.

It was the stone rejected by the builders
that became the keystone.
This was the Lord's doing
and it is wonderful to see?'

And they would have liked to arrest him, because they realised that the parable was aimed at them, but they were afraid of the crowds. So they left him alone and went away.

(Mark 12:1–12)

As in so many of Jesus' stories, the impact of this story depends on a knowledge of the Old Testament roots and references of what he is saying. His audience, particularly the religious leaders against whom the story is told, would immediately have recognized what Jesus was doing: it was a well established trick of the teaching trade. He was taking an Old Testament story, which has a very strong 'line', and giving it a new twist. In this way he could remind them of the original point of the Old Testament reference, and add his own commentary on it.

This story is unusual in that he does it twice. He sketches very quickly a prophecy from Isaiah (ch. 5), gives it a substantial new meaning and the account of the son – 'They will respect my son' – and then finishes with another Old Testament reference that both encapsulates and enlarges the point of the whole story. So we have here much to work on: we will uncover it layer by layer.

Clearly the story is about God's last offer to the people of Israel, often portrayed as a vine or vineyard in the Old Testament. In desperation, God sends his son. Surely that will work. They may beat up the prophets and behead John the Baptist, but they will treat the son with respect. But no. They reject him. But what is the 'share of the produce of the vineyard' the son was supposed to collect? It is almost inconceivable that the 'chief priests, and the scribes and the elders' would not connect this with the end of the parent-story in Isaiah 5:

> Yes, the vineyard of Yahweh Sabaoth
> is the house of Israel,
> and the men of Judah
> that chosen plant.
> He expected justice, but found bloodshed,
> integrity, but only a cry of distress. (Isaiah 5:7)

The son had come to collect justice and integrity, the fruits of a loving relationship with Yahweh. And all the vineyard had yielded was 'sour grapes' (Isaiah 5:4). Notice how direct and 'earthy' is this reference. Justice and integrity are not other-worldly concepts in the Old Testament: indeed the editor of Isaiah continues with a fierce prophecy against the rich.

> Woe to those who add house to house
> and join field to field
> until everywhere belongs to them
> and they are the sole inhabitants of the land.

> (Isaiah 5:8)

We must be faithful, then, to the political reference in this central story. God offers his people love, and expects a response which will both enable and incorporate justice. The offer is rejected and the expectation disappointed. There is more . . .

In an almost outrageous way, Jesus changes the end of Isaiah's story. In that, the vineyard is destroyed. In Jesus' version, however, the vineyard is taken away and given to others. And to drive the point home, Jesus quotes from Psalm 118, a remarkable choice.

First, it is a processional hymn about God's love for his people. Jesus is repeating the theme that is as crucial to him as it was to the Old Testament prophets. Second, he is using a messianic reference, well established in the Old Testament, and applying it almost directly to himself, and absolutely directly to the present situation. Third, he is quoting from a Psalm which contains exactly the liturgical greetings that people (the common people, the poor) had shouted at him as he entered Jerusalem only two days earlier. Fourth, he is warning the religious establishment that they will reject their own messiah.

No wonder they wanted to silence him! He threatens them at every point. Their political life is corrupt, untransformed and incapable of transformation because they have allowed the love affair to become institutionalized. And here is this carpenter's lad claiming that the messianic moment has arrived and that if they fail to respond to it in love and joy – even respond to *him*, for goodness sake – the special calling of Israel will be passed to 'others'. How scandalous! . . . The man's mad. Clearly not to be taken seriously. . . . Better put him away, just in case. . . .

St Mark tells us, however, that the common people, having greeted him as Messiah two days ago, still supported him. Of course. They supported him because they sensed the truth of his oblique criticisms of their leaders' corruption. They sensed the possibilities of the Kingdom that the messiah would establish. Although they misunderstood the foundation of the Kingdom – a courageous, trustful love for Yahweh – they pined for a social and religious order that had more integrity than their own.

It might be a good idea now to reread the story a couple

of times, alert to what it would be saying to a reasonably well educated (i.e. well schooled in the Old Testament) bystander. . . .

¶Watch the chief priests and elders wander off, muttering and scowling over their shoulders. There is Jesus, quietly watching them go. Go up to him, and ask him about 'the others . . .' If not Israel, who . . . ? Who is the Kingdom for . . . ?

It is important to give yourself plenty of time now. Don't be tempted to rush on. Let the conversation develop if it will. . . . Draw into the conversation, if it seems appropriate, some of the common people. How do they react to this story? . . . Who do they think 'the others' are? . . . Watch Jesus talking with them. . . . Ask him why he thinks the Kingdom will be rejected. . . .

When you have gone as far as you can with that, reflect on any of the stories in chapter 4 – or, much better, one of your own discovery – in the light of the conversation you have just had. . . . What emerges from that about the coming of the Kingdom today?

It is good if you can talk over what comes alive for you in this exercise with a few others who have also done it. You may well be surprised how different are the accounts you bring. That is nothing to worry about . . . What matters is whether, having wrestled with this, you are better able to stand alongside the poor in the presence of God and offer him the quality of love he offers you.

The Kingdom described

Jesus offers in his person a final chance to the Jews – a chance to enter a Covenant love that will transform their lives at every level. That love will make possible the reality of God's reign, and will therefore inaugurate the Kingdom.

As though to tempt them to let go of their idolatries and false securities, Jesus tells them what the Kingdom will be like. There is much of this descriptive material, especially in the synoptic Gospels, but I have chosen the Beatitudes for our next exercise because they are the most powerful short summary of how Jesus tried to seduce the people to fall in love with God the Father.

> Seeing the crowds, he went up the hill. There he sat down and was joined by his disciples. Then he began to speak. This is what he taught them:
>
> > 'How happy are the poor in spirit;
> > theirs is the kingdom of heaven.
> > Happy the gentle:
> > they shall have the earth for their heritage.
> > Happy those who mourn;
> > they shall be comforted.
> > Happy those who hunger and thirst for what is right:
> > they shall be satisfied.
> > Happy the merciful:
> > they shall have mercy shown them.
> > Happy the pure in heart:
> > they shall see God.
> > Happy the peacemakers:
> > they shall be called sons of God.
> > Happy those who are persecuted in the cause of right:
> > theirs is the kingdom of heaven.
>
> 'Happy are you when people abuse you and persecute you and speak all kinds of calumny against you on my account. Rejoice and be glad, for your reward will be great in heaven; this is how they persecuted the prophets before you.'
>
> (Matthew 5:1–12)

¶Read this passage through again, this time substituting for 'How happy are . . .' the words which are in some ways truer to the real meaning: 'You are in the right place when you are . . .'

How differently do you react to this familiar passage when you make that substitution? . . . It is important to reflect on that. . . .

Why? The Chinese noun for crisis, so I am told, is a combination of two words, which translate as 'danger' and 'opportunity'. We have both those elements here. The dangers are obvious. Being in the 'right place' implies being poor, gentle, mourning, merciful, peaceable and persecuted – in other words, powerless, weak and vulnerable. How can that possibly be the 'right place'? It is the right place because it makes no claims on anyone, not even on God. And it is then that God's offer of love and wholeness, for the individual and the community, can be accepted. As it is accepted so the richness of the offer is revealed.

It is hard for us, inured by repetition and cut off from the cultural roots of the Gospels, to comprehend just how astonishing are the promises contained in the Beatitudes. Although nearly all of them have clear Old Testament roots, they would have been shocking to the religious establishment of the day. To promise to anyone that they would see God was blasphemous. To offer the Kingdom of Heaven or sonship of God to the poor and the persecuted was almost worse. These were honours that even the great patriarchs would hardly aspire to; and here was this brash young man scattering them round like confetti to the riff-raff.

Precisely. That is the nature of the Kingdom. Its richness of relationship and transformative energy is offered to those who have no claims on it, but who are capable of receiving gratuity because they live by gratuity. Look again at the list of 'right places'. It makes a perfect description of what it means to live by gratuity – to live out the loving generosity of the King and his Kingdom.

A paradox then. The blessings of the Kingdom will fall on those who live by the Kingdom! That takes us back to the crisis. The Kingdom is a crisis both in the Chinese sense of dangerous opportunity and in the Greek sense of judgement. If we choose to try to live by gratuity, we shall be enabled to do so by the transforming love of God; but if we refuse even to try, even to *want* to try, then we condemn ourselves to the untransformed life of the human condition.

The Kingdom then is about choice. That is not a new development. In the Old Testament, Israel is constantly presented with the choice of a loving trustfulness in Yahweh – or in idols. What is new here is the inversion of the order of transformation. 'Be my people and I will make you free and whole' is Yahweh's offer in the Old Testament. But Christ turns that round. 'Live as though you were free and whole, and God will adopt you as his children – and make you free and whole.'

Again it is important to see how revolutionary this offer must have sounded to Jesus' critics. Not one of the Beatitudes is overtly 'religious': they say nothing explicitly (arguably everything implicity) about the Law, about Temple worship, about the sacrificial system of 'getting right with God.' The deliberateness with which Jesus makes this point is almost brutal. Verse 6 ('those who hunger and thirst for what is right') is a quotation from Isaiah 51:1. But Isaiah has a poetic parallel: 'Listen to me, you who pursue integrity, who seek Yahweh. . . .' Jesus drops the parallel with its overtly 'religious' reference and concentrates on the search for integrity, for what is right. The common currency of institutionalized religious life is simply ignored. It is as though Jesus is saying: 'Forget all that stuff. Try to open yourselves to the suffering of the world and respond to it in love. Then you will find God among you, and you will experience at first hand the quality of his love.'

Hence the play on the word 'poor' – 'You are in the right place when you are poor'. Matthew, unlike Luke, adds 'in spirit'. That does not remove the richness of the word – rather it reinforces the central notion of claimlessness. Those who accept they have no claims on God (through their religiosity or abundance of good works) and no claims on society (through their wealth, power or prestige); it is they who are in the right place to let God rule their lives and to be transformed in the process.

¶To let all this settle, the exercise on this passage is in two parts. First, go through the Beatitudes, reading 'You are in the right place' for 'Happy . . .' and ask God to show you your life and the life of your parish or community in that perspective. . . . Ask him to help you think if you are in the right place . . . to let you see where you might be. . . . Try to avoid judging yourself or selves; above all do not be harsh with yourself. . . . Let God show you what he wants you to see.

The second part of the exercise is to go through the list again, still in 'You are in the right place . . .' mode. Identify people or groups or communities who seem to be in the right place. . . . You may find the stories in chapter 4 helpful here, as pointers to the 'right places' where some people are. When you have identified them, a *thinking* process, stand alongside them before God, a *meditative* or feeling state. . . . Most people find it hard to make that switch, from the head to the heart, from analysis to offering, from mental activity to stillness. It is the essence of prayer . . . and it comes with practice! So keep trying: just stand there, in the right place with the right people. . . . You may want to end the exercise with a word of thanksgiving.

If the Beatitudes describe the essence of the Kingdom in terms of the sea-change in values and perceptions that is involved, our next meditation, based on a parable that is unique to Mark, makes it clear that the coming of the Kingdom depends on the invisible but unstoppable processes of God.

> He also said, 'This is what the kingdom of God is like. A man throws seed on the land. Night and day, while he sleeps, when he is awake, the seed is sprouting and growing; how, he does not know. Of its own accord the land produces first the shoot, then the ear, then the full grain in the ear. And when the crop is ready, he loses no time: he starts to reap because the harvest has come.'
>
> (Mark 4:26–9)

This parable holds in tension two fundamental aspects of the coming of the Kingdom: that it depends on the power of God; and that it demands decisive, resolute action at the appropriate time from men and women.

The seed grows night and day, untended by the farmer. He is irrelevant to the process once he has sown the seed. 'Of its own accord', the soil sustains the germinating seed, which grows with a life of its own, thrusting upwards towards light and warmth. The farmer remains irrelevant. For the power at work is both mysterious and fundamental. It is the basis of all life.

St Mark evidently thought this worth emphasizing. Not

only does he alone use this story, but he follows it with a parable that makes the same point – the mustard seed growing by a secret power to be 'the biggest shrub of them all' – and then, as if finally to ram it home, by the remarkable story of the calming of the storm. That ends with the words, in which it is easy to catch the awe and tingling excitement: 'Even the wind and sea obey him.' Here, St Mark is saying, is the power of God at work, and it is incarnated in Jesus. It is that power, made present in that person, which is at work bringing the Kingdom.

It is helpful to relate this to our earlier discussion of guilt, powerlessness and hyperactivism. Guilt is irrelevant at one level because although we may often get in the way, like a lump of concrete sitting on top of the germinating seed, the power of God is greater than any impediment we can throw in the way. Powerlessness is irrelevant because what matters is the power God chooses to exercise in the establishment of his Kingdom. And hyperactivism is a not very subtle form of pride because it stems from the odd belief that our efforts can substitute for the power of God. What a clot a farmer would appear who felt inadequate because his wheat took three weeks to germinate, powerless because it took six months to reach maturity, underoccupied if he was not forever fussing over it.

But there is a tension in the story between this period of growth, of preparation on the one hand and the decisive, irreversible action demanded of the farmer once harvest day has come. Now a plan of action and hard work are essential.

In Jesus' teaching, this tension is easily understood. The power of God had been at work in the history of Israel, but now in his person the moment of decisive action had arrived. The harvest, often used as a symbol of the messianic crisis, was here.

It is important, but not easy, to disentangle two quite separate issues. At one level, we can read this parable in the sense that Jesus most probably intended his audience to take it – as a story about the need to respond to God's power manifested in Jesus. The decision is then to accept Jesus as the messiah. But at another level, it is a story about co-operation with the power of God at work in the world. Then the issue is that of judgement, of discernment: when is the appropriate time? What is the appropriate action? How can the fulfilment of God's purposes be best secured?

In our exercise and prayer on this passage, we shall concentrate on these two aspects: the unseen power of God at work in the world; and the need for discernment in co-operating with that power.

¶Start by thinking of all the ways in which you have seen the creative power of God at work in the natural world; in plants, animals, people; in tissue growth as a wound heals; in landscape and seascape; in changing seasons, . . . Then try to do the same for the psychic world: creation, recreation and healing in human consciousness. . . . Then think of that same power at work in personal relationships: people falling in love; parents and children experiencing an evolving relationship from dependence to independence to inverse dependence as the parents become helpless; deepening relationships in a community that slowly learns to cope with conflict and grow out of it. . . . Finally, can you think of the power of God at work in history? This is such a vast theme, you will find it becomes handleable only if you reflect on one topic; I find helpful taking the treatment of racial minorities, or workers, or women, or prisoners of war. (Don't fall for either a simplistic 'It's all getting better'; nor for a 'It's just as ghastly as it always was, only better disguised'. Remember you are trying to perceive the power of God at work, not to judge its pace or its 'effectiveness'.)

It is important to keep the analytical part of this exercise in check – or you could end up rewriting the *Encyclopaedia Britannica!* What is required is to bring to consciousness the sense of a power at work 'behind' superficial phenomena. The meditative part of the exercise is to open ourselves, 'ally' ourselves with this power, to become so aware of it that even in our darkest moments we can trust it – literally with our lives . . .

Find a deep silence within you . . . become aware of that power at the heart of the silence. . . .

The second theme is that of discernment; how can we discern the appropriate time and action? Reading the signs of the times and matching action to those signs are near the heart of living out the Gospel. No surprise, then, that this is a notoriously difficult area, and one in which well-intentioned people can make genuine mistakes. Indeed that is what makes Christian obedience so conflict-laden and anxiety-provoking: there are no certainties and two people possessed of the same depth of spiritual perception may well differ. Paul and Barnabas are alive and well, and living in many religious communities.

Inevitably, then, we have to acknowledge the centrality of humility in our discernment of the signs of the times. Maybe we are misguided. Maybe the others see it more clearly than we do. How hard we find that to contemplate, and how easily we assume that those who read the signs differently from us are lacking in faith or perception or courage. And our difficulty is enhanced by the fact that they may be! Humility does not mean becoming a door mat, allowing everyone to walk all over us. God may indeed have revealed more to us than to them – but we had better start by assuming the converse.

We shall not discern the signs nor the appropriate actions if we are in a state of inner turmoil. No one goes out to harvest the grain in the midst of a storm. Nor should we. The securing and maintenance of a core of deep tranquillity through periods of imageless meditation is essential if we are to sharpen our faculties of discernment. That is not easy – and if you are unfamiliar with them you may find 'centring' exercises helpful. These are described in many books on meditation: I like Anthony de Mello's *Sadhana: A way to God*.

Third, any farmer will tell you that the temptation is always to start the harvest too soon. The weather is fair; the ear has fallen till it is nearly touching the stalk: Let's go. The wise farmer waits another day or two, knowing that residual moisture will ruin the grain in storage. Wait. Wait. How hard that is. When I had a farm in Zambia, where the weather was predictable, waiting to start the harvest was a period of stress and tension. So it is in the spiritual life – where the weather is anything but predictable.

Fourth, once harvest starts, you put everything you have into it. You have one objective: to get the grain out of the field and into the silo. In much the same way, when discerning the signs of the times and fitting the action to them, we have to put the reign of God at the heart of our thinking. There can be no room for secondary motives, compromises, sectional interests or defence of bits of our selves that we would rather not throw into the struggle. Shortly before I was asked to resign as Director of Christian Aid, I caused offence by saying that those of us who purport to take seriously the biblical call to justice had much to learn from those who go to prison for the sake of peace. Discernment brooks no comfortable compromise. 'The love that moves and causes one to choose must descend from above, that is, from the love of God. So before one chooses, he should perceive that the greater or less attachment for the object of his choice is solely because of his Creator and Lord,' says St Ignatius in his Spiritual Exercises. And the emphasis is on 'solely'.

Lastly, one does not go into the harvest field with nail scissors or a hat stand. One goes with the most appropriate and efficient tools at one's command. Harvest is a serious business: it determines whether or not the farm can survive. It is hard, sweaty work that taxes physical strength and endurance to the limit. Important, then, to take the best implements you can find. And use them with a will. There is no room for tokenism, for fine speeches, for endless committees, for referring decisions up long hierarchies and then down again. Least of all is there room for inaction, idleness or pseudo-activity that masks an unwillingness to get stuck in. 'Ah, but the world of the spirit is not a farm,' says the voice of caution. No doubt, but Jesus did not choose this parable for an agricultural society without being confident of the closeness of the parallel.

¶Humility, tranquillity, patience, clarity and appropriateness: those are some of the keys of discernment. They are also, of course, keys to the whole of the spiritual life. No one exercise will put them in our hands. To complete this meditation, however, I would like you to fantasize that you are a farmer waiting to start the harvest. Your son wants to start now. . . . You are sure that you should wait another two or three days. . . . Let the fantasy develop. . . . Then move to your own situation, both personal and corporate. Don't try to analyse it now . . . Just let it sit in your consciousness as you pray for humility . . . for tranquillity . . . for patience . . . for grace to keep the service of God central and unalloyed . . . for wisdom to choose appropriate means. . . .

The Kingdom enacted

The Kingdom is offered and described. Because deeds speak louder and deeper than words, however, the Kingdom is also enacted. Many of Jesus' *acts* are prophetic demonstrations of the new life, the new quality of life, that the Kingdom offers. They are both a foretaste and a summary of the kind of living the love-affair which God makes possible – and inevitable. In that sense they run in parallel with the parabolic teaching ministry: both teaching and acting are seductive glimpses into the joyful transformation that the love-affair involves. Both state, with the subtlety and gentleness that invite trust rather than obedience: '*This* is what it could be like, if only . . .'

The most obvious example is the healing ministry of Jesus. For here the direct confrontation with the universal forces of evil – of destruction and diminishment – is played out in public, presented in sharp, unambiguous terms. The people and their religious leaders must make of it what they will. Almost inevitably, the latter decide that Jesus is in league with the forces of evil, for they cannot make room for him in their neat systematization of the love of God; while the former, the people, are not very sure what to think. On balance, they prefer to be left to stew in their own misery-making juices rather than face up to the wild challenges of the love of God.

They reached the country of the Gerasenes on the other side of the lake, and no sooner had he left the boat than a man with an unclean spirit came out from the tombs towards him. The man lived in the tombs and no one could secure him any more, even with a chain; because he had often been secured with fetters and chains but had snapped the chains and broken the fetters, and no one had the strength to control him. All night and all day, among the tombs and in the mountains, he would howl and gash himself with stones. Catching sight of Jesus from a distance, he ran up and fell at his feet and shouted at the top of his voice, 'What do you want with me, Jesus, son of the Most

High God? Swear by God you will not torture me!' – For Jesus had been saying to him, 'Come out of the man, unclean spirit.' 'What is your name?' Jesus asked. 'My name is legion,' he answered, 'for there are many of us.' And he begged him earnestly not to send them out of the district. Now there was there on the mountainside a great herd of pigs feeding, and the unclean spirits begged him, 'Send us to the pigs, let us go into them.' So he gave them leave. With that, the unclean spirits came out and went into the pigs, and the herd of about two thousand pigs charged down the cliff into the lake, and there they were drowned. The swineherds ran off and told their story in the town and in the country round about; and the people came to see what had really happened. They came to Jesus and saw the demoniac sitting there, clothed and in his full senses – the very man who had had the legion in him before – and they were afraid. And those who had witnessed it reported what had happened to the demoniac and what had become of the pigs. Then they began to implore Jesus to leave the neighbourhood. As he was getting into a boat, the man who had been possessed begged to be allowed to stay with him. Jesus would not let him but said to him, 'Go home to your people and tell them all that the Lord in his mercy has done for you.' So the man went off and proceeded to spread throughout the Decapolis all that Jesus had done for him. And everyone was amazed.

(Mark 5:1–20)

Following immediately the calming of the storm, this story is the first of three healing miracles; the teaching of the Kingdom, then, is followed by its enactment. Its placing here is significant: it is as though St Mark is emphasizing the symbolic load that this story carries.

Clearly the wretched demoniac is heavily symbolic (by which I do not mean to impugn the historical basis of the story). That symbolism is given special emphasis by the detailed description of his symptoms: he lives among the tombs (and is therefore ritually unclean); he identifies with the forces of death and decay; he is ungovernable, even physically out of control, the object, then, of disintegration; he is hugely strong since the powers of death and disintegration defy description in their ferocity. He destroys himself – richly symbolic, since the forces of evil usually seek the co-operation of what they would destroy. Above all, he is 'legion' – so far advanced in the process of disintegration that the principle of unity, of wholeness, has been overpowered and he is literally coming apart as a recognizable person.

A symbol, then, of everything that makes a joyful union with God the father impossible, he nonetheless recognizes the nature of Jesus and his healing. Jesus is the implacable foe of everything that destroys, divides and dis-eases this wretched man: the 'unclean spirits' expect him to 'torture' them. There can be no compromise, no easy letting off the hook. Unclean to unclean, they are 'allowed' to possess the pigs in a final act of self-destruction.

In our society where animals are sometimes preferred to people, there is some resistance to the idea of the pigs being made the vehicles for the destruction of the spirits. Seen from the perspective of the swineherds, it must certainly have seemed unjust and ruinous. That, however, is to miss the *scale* of the event: it is rather like a barmaid complaining when an opera star shatters a wineglass in the midst of a climactic aria. This was indeed the climax of a cosmic opera: the public and highly physical enfleshment of the power of the Kingdom of God over the disintegrative forces of evil. The very fact that there were two thousand pigs (perhaps merely a symbolic way of saying a huge number) emphasizes how far the disintegration had gone, and therefore how grand was the scale of the healing.

Notice, finally, the reaction of the people. First, they simply do not believe – they had to come to see what 'had really happened'. When they begin to grasp the order of the transformation that had actually occurred, they were, second, afraid. And third, they want nothing of it. This latter reaction should not surprise us. I was once asked by a senior British diplomat to evaluate a rural development scheme in the Caribbean run jointly by Rastafarians and Christians. 'Can't make it out, Elliott' said the diplomat, 'They give away what they don't need. And when I asked them what it was all in aid of, d'you know what they said? "It's all for love, man, all for love". My God, Elliott, if that gets around, there's no knowing where it will end.' There is nothing so threatening as a radical challenge to our secure values.

¶The exercise based on this passage is in three parts. First, try to build a 'pyramid of suffering'. Start with individuals who, like the demoniac, are being torn apart – first by physical suffering, then by psychic suffering. Take one individual you know personally from each category and see him or her as a symbol of the forces of evil and of what those forces do to people. Then move on to a small community – the community in which you live, your parish, your office – and identify the disintegrative power at work there. Then your local political unit – city, state, local council. . . . What is tearing that apart? Then move on to your nation . . . Where do you see 'legion' there? What are the deep, under-the-surface agents of destructiveness? And, finally, look at the whole globe . . . with the same questions.

Move now from analysis to contemplation. Stand quietly behind Christ as he confronts those forces – 'Come out, unclean spirit . . .'

Many people who do this exercise find that as they contemplate Christ they become aware of the forces of disintegration in themselves: their 'standing alongside Christ' in the cosmic struggle is both a blessing – their 'right place' – but also a judgement. For how can I take the side of Christ in so elemental a struggle when I am the seat of what he is struggling against?

The second exercise, then, offers our 'legion' for Christ's healing. Back to the pigs. There they are, a great herd of them; and there is Christ telling my legion to be gone . . . and the pigs start, one by one, to run down the field and over the cliff. There goes my pride . . . there my anger . . . there my love of money . . . there my lust . . . there my possessiveness. . . . You will almost certainly want to end this part of the exercise with thanksgiving. . . .

The third part of the exercise follows naturally from the first two. Christ says to you: 'Go home to your people and tell them all that the Lord in his mercy has done for you.' What do you tell them, in the light of the first part of this exercise? . . . and then in the light of the second?

The imagery in the last story was powerful; note the contrast between the demoniac sitting among the tombs slashing himself with a sharp stone and the healed man fully dressed talking quietly to Jesus. *Contrast* lies at the heart of the Gospel: the contrast between the enslaving legalisms of orthodox Judaism and the liberating life of the Kingdom. St John's Gospel is full of these contrasts – for example light and darkness – as he widens the perspective from the world of Judaism to the cosmic plane. Our next exercise brings together the contrast offered by the Kingdom; judgement on the 'old' religious life; and the abundance of life offered at the cosmic level.

> Three days later there was a wedding at Cana in Galilee. The mother of Jesus was there, and Jesus and his disciples had also been invited. When they ran out of wine, since the wine provided for the wedding was all finished, the mother of Jesus said to him, 'They have no wine'. Jesus said, 'Woman, why turn to me? My hour has not come yet.' His mother said to the servants, 'Do whatever he tells you.' There were six stone water jars standing there meant for the ablutions that are customary among the Jews: each could hold twenty or thirty gallons. Jesus said to the servants, 'Fill the jars with water,' and they filled them to the brim. 'Draw some out now', he told them, 'and take it to the steward.' They did this; the steward tasted the water, and it had turned into wine. Having no idea where it came from – only the servants who had drawn the water knew – the steward called the bridegroom and said, 'People generally serve the best wine first, and keep the cheaper sort till the guests have had plenty to drink; but you have kept the best wine till now.'

> (John 2:1–10)

Here we have three levels of transformation; each is relevant to our theme. At its simplest, the story is about changing water into wine. Even at that level, however, there is a richness of allusion that deserves attention. Water was a sign of God's Covenant love in the Old Testament – a fact recorded in Exodus, celebrated in the Psalms, and repeated in one of the great historical liturgies of Deuteronomy: 'Do not then

forget Yahweh your God . . . who in this waterless place
[the desert] brought you water from the hardest rock . . .'
(Deuteronomy 8:14–15). Water then, is the symbol of
salvation, the embodiment of God's loving care for his people.
It is also, and in a sense derivatively, a sign and means of
purity. For it is the pure in heart who will respond to God's
offer of salvation. According to St John, however, Christ takes
this symbol and transforms it into wine, a symbol of the final
banquet foreseen in contemporary Jewish eschatology. The
contrast then is between the salvation offered by the Law and
Temple worship on the one hand; and on the other, the heady,
intoxicating possibilities of reconciliation and transformation
offered by Christ. That offer points to the *eschaton*, the end of
time; but is here and now. The Kingdom is on offer now, and
yet it is the Kingdom of the final transformation of all things.

At a more allegorical level, the story is about the supersession of Jewish purity rites by the gratuity of the Kingdom.
It is significant that Christ chose the water of the purification
ceremony and turned it into wine that people, already well
supped, would drink. The Kingdom is less concerned about
outer purity; it is about the abundance of joy and gaiety that
is symbolized by the easy fellowship and harmony of a good
party. (It is worth remembering just how much wine Christ
offered. The quantity and quality are symbols of the radical
difference between external cleansing and change in inner
values.)

Finally, at the deepest level, St John has in mind the
institution of the Eucharist, significantly at the very start of
his account of Jesus' ministry. For St John, the cosmic revolution that Christ represents is centred firmly in the cross. All
that Cana signifies is achieved only through the self-offering
love that took Christ to the cross. In that sense, the new era
of the coming of the Kingdom is dependent on suffering love.
'The hour' for that to be lived out has not yet come, but this
first miracle is a straw-in-the-wind, a foretaste of the cost of
transformation.

We have here, then, a story of the profoundest meaning.
Like the healing stories of the synoptic Gospels, it proclaims
the offer of the Kingdom, not only in contrast to the brittle
dryness of an externalized Judaism, but also in contrast to
the conventions of the world. 'People generally . . . but you

. . .' Christ and his cross mark the point at which the radical break with both the past and the conventional present is made. Abundant, superb wine is there for the taking: but only those who recognize the significance of Christ will taste it. The central theme of our exercise is transformation.

¶First, imagine yourself to be a guest at the wedding, perhaps a relative of the groom. You are aware that the wine is running out, and of the embarrassment that is going to cause . . . You see Mary speak with Jesus; you hear her say something about the wine . . . he looks a little uncomfortable, as though undecided . . . then he speaks to the servants . . . you notice nothing more till a slave brings a new jug of wine to your table. You ask where it came from. He tells you. Others overhear: 'He changed the water in the purification jars to wine – *this* wine.' Some at your table laugh; some abuse the slave . . . how do you react? . . . Go up to Jesus and ask him what he has done . . . and why? Ask him what it means. . . . Listen carefully to the answer . . . take your time . . .

Most people who do this exercise find that what comes to them of the significance of what they have taken part in, albeit in imagination, has much to do with newness; a radical change; a new beginning; a costly but more rewarding relationship between God and man, not only at the individual levels, but also at the cosmic level. 'Things can never be the same again,' was how one retreatant aptly put it. Sure. But that process is at work here and now.

¶The second part of our meditation, therefore, is to look for transformation at work among us. Where is it true to say that 'Things can never be the same again?' No one finds this an easy question to ask of themselves: indeed it can be dangerous and/or destructive. If it seems helpful, I do not want to discourage you from applying this question to yourself: I would, however, suggest that you do not spend too long on this. Rather I want you to apply it to your community, your local political unit and your nation. Where is it possible to see water being changed into wine? Where is the old order giving way to new possibilities? Or, to change the metaphor, where are there signs of spring in the values, perceptions, world-views of those around us?

There is a great temptation to cheat in this exercise! How easy to see the process of transformation where we *want* to see it, to resort, in other words, to ideological buttressing. It is important, therefore, to be asked to be *shown* answers to the questions in the last paragraph, rather than impose them on God. For the question we are really asking is about God's activity in the world: where is he at work? Where are the growing points of the Kingdom?

We need, then, to combine a critical, analytical mind – God does not talk nonsense – with a humble, listening inner ear. Most people find that an extraordinarily difficult combination to pull off: we leave either our minds at the church door or our humility at the study door. Perhaps the easiest way through is to alternate periods of imageless 'listening', of expectant waiting; with periods of conscious mental probing in which we 'test the spirits' . . . There are obvious advantages to doing this exercise in a group. Members of the group will produce different and conflicting 'answers'. That is neither surprising nor alarming. What matters is not that everyone comes up with the same 'answer', but that everyone learns to *look* for the process of transformation in their own place.

If you do this exercise on your own, you may find it helpful to think yourself into the skin of someone, whether an acquaintance or a public figure, with whose politics you cannot agree. If they were doing this exercise, as conscientiously and as 'openly' as you, where do you think they would come out? . . . Clearly they are not more 'right' or less 'right' than you. Perceptions of the working of God are never easy or unambiguous. (Remember the reactions at your table at Cana). Sooner or later, we have to make a commitment of faith: 'Yes, I believe that God is at work in the peace movement . . . in feminism . . . in the rising consciousness of global poverty. . . .'

¶When you are ready, the final part of this exercise is to offer what you have 'seen' or 'heard' of God's transforming activity in thanksgiving – and in obedience.

That last is important – even if it sounds a bit old fashioned.

If the wine of the cross is 'there', where you think it is, the expectation of a response is over-powering. . . . Let it overpower you. . . . This kind of prayer is not an academic exercise: do not be surprised, or afraid, therefore if you find it calls from you a response that is itself a transformation.

In the last exercise, we saw the Kingdom of God as a process of radical transformation for the whole life, for the whole cosmos. In this exercise, we pursue that insight of St John, and take it a step further and deeper.

The setting is the raising of Lazarus. Jesus has deliberately, or so it seems, delayed his return to Bethany, even though he was told Lazarus was critically ill. Some of his disciples would prefer him not to go at all, as the last time he was there the Jews turned on him and nearly killed him. Finally convinced that Lazarus is dead, Jesus sets out 'to wake him'.

On arriving, Jesus found that Lazarus had been in the tomb for four days already. Bethany is only about two miles from Jerusalem, and many Jews had come to Martha and Mary to sympathise with them over their brother. When Martha heard that Jesus had come she went to meet him. Mary remained sitting in the house. Martha said to Jesus, 'If you had been here, my brother would not have died, but I know that, even now, whatever you ask of God, he will grant you.' 'Your brother' said Jesus to her 'will rise again.' Martha said, 'I know he will rise again at the resurrection on the last day'. Jesus said:

I am the resurrection,
If anyone believes in me, even though he dies he will live,
and whoever lives and believes in me
will never die.
Do you believe this?

'Yes, Lord,' she said 'I believe that you are the Christ, the Son of God, the one who was to come into this world.'

When she had said this, she went and called her sister Mary, saying in a low voice, 'The Master is here and wants

to see you'. Hearing this, Mary got up quickly and went
to him.

(John 11:17–29)

A constant but so far unemphasized theme in these exercises
has been rejection and suffering. The last of the Beatitudes
(arguably inserted later or from a different oral tradition)
describes, as in a right place, those who are persecuted. Jesus
was thrown out of Gerasa. The wedding at Cana portends
the cross. As a hidden melody, the music within the music,
rejection, suffering and death are ever present in Jesus'
ministry.

For the proclamation of the Kingdom is intolerable. It
threatens too many established interests, too many self-securi-
ties, too many idols. It opens a new campaign in the great
cosmic drama of love, and as such is met by hatred, fear,
violence and destruction.

To St John, with his mystic's consciousness of the univer-
sality of Christ's life and death, the raising of Lazarus is a
demonstration that these negative reactions are not to be
taken as final or cosmically definitive. For the life that Christ
offers – a recurrent theme in the fourth Gospel – transcends
even death itself. Here St John combines both an acted
parable and direct teaching to drive the point home. 'I am
the resurrection . . .' The contrast is made explicit. Belief
(which for St John is courageous trust rather than intellectual
assent) in Christ will ensure that life is brought out of the
most destructive environment – and not just life as an abstraction, but the full, abundant, vibrant life that St John sees at
the heart of the cosmic adventure.

In a sense, then, the wheel has turned full circle. Offered
the possibility of life transformed, Israel spurned it, making
the calling of the Suffering Servant inevitable. The Servant
however, guarantees life in all its fullness, despite shared
suffering, to those who choose it by giving him their trust.
Here is the offer of love made from the far side of suffering.

Notice that Jesus does not seem particularly impressed by
Martha's religious platitude that Lazarus will rise from the
dead 'on the last day'. He does not say: 'That's quite right,
dear Martha. You believe in me and Lazarus will be all right
at the end of time.' He says something far stronger. 'Have

courageous trust in what I represent, the breaking-in of the Kingdom, and you will be so transformed that physical death will be irrelevant to you.' No wonder Martha is snapped out of conventional religious pieties, into a statement that would have guaranteed her death by stoning if it had been heard by any orthodox Jew. No wonder, too, that Mary is in such a hurry to go and speak to Jesus. That is where the first part of this exercise begins.

¶Think of yourself as Mary. You are sitting at home, mourning the death of Lazarus with some friends from Jerusalem. You tell them that if only Jesus had come in time. . . . They are sympathetic but sceptical. . . . Then Martha arrives, flushed, excited, strangely alive. . . . She whispers to you that Jesus is half a mile down the road, asking for you. . . . Martha presses your arm and says in a breath tense with meaning: 'It's going to be all right'. . . . You get up quickly and start down the road. . . . Make that short journey in your imagination. What are you thinking . . . expecting . . . ?

You meet Jesus. What do you say to him? . . . What does he say to you . . . Stay with him for the rest of the day . . . especially when he raises Lazarus and immediately afterwards. . . . Talk to him about it.

This can be a powerful exercise, so do not be surprised if more is released than you can comfortably handle. Take from it what you can appropriate and come back to the rest some time later.

I hope the exercise will enable you to grasp something of the *scale* of the 'sign' that Jesus gives. The Kingdom is majestic in its comprehensiveness. It is not a matter of a little more of this or a little less of that. Christ in neither a fastidious cook nor a social engineer. The Kingdom he proclaims goes to the heart of life itself and makes possible an order of transformation that only a resurrection story can adequately symbolize.

It is the grandeur of this order of transformation that I want you to put at the heart of your meditation in the second part of this exercise.

¶Taking the raising of Lazarus as a symbol of the power of

love in action for the Kingdom, bring to Christ *one* area of conflict, impoverishment, 'world problem'. It may be the arms race or war in a particular region or economic injustice or disregard for the environment – or it may be something quite different. . . . Whatever it is, avoid switching into analytical mode. . . . Rather take it as a whole tangle of unresolved questions, difficulties – almost literally a can of worms, writhingly intertwined in their stinking unattractiveness – and lay it at Christ's feet, saying with Martha: 'I believe that you are the Christ, the Son of God, who was to come into the world.' . . . If you are familiar with techniques of meditative prayer that use a mantra, you might like to shorten that declaration, perhaps to: 'Come into this world . . .', and use it as a mantra. . . . It is important, however, to be alert throughout the time you spend on this prayer to the transformative possibilities of the Kingdom. It is in that faith that such a prayer makes sense . . . 'Come into this world. . . . and transform it utterly . . .'

The Kingdom rejected – and reoffered

The Kingdom received

In chapter 6 we have seen the Kingdom offered, described
and lived out. We must now look at the reception it receives.
We have, of course, already touched on this, explicitly in the
first and last exercises of chapter 6. Now we must enter more
deeply into the human condition that makes the proclamation
of the Kingdom divisive and conflictual. For there is no cheap
peace or guaranteed harmony when the full grandeur of the
Kingdom is apprehended. It blows families, communities and
churches to bits – which may explain the eagerness with
which the latter seek to tame it. Those who live for the
Kingdom cannot therefore expect, in this pre-partum period,
to be spared conflict of the most painful and sometimes cruel
kind. Recall again the stories of chapter 4. Each of those
people has experienced the Kingdom more as a sword than
as a dove.

The story on which this exercise is based makes the same
point, but, as it were, from the other end of the telescope. We
are conditioned to think in terms of the preference of both
Old Testament and New for the poor and powerless. Rightly
so. But we sometimes overlook the radicality of the offer
of the Kingdom. Like the parable of the Good Samaritan,
systematically misunderstood – and thereby castrated – as it
is, this story reminds us that the Kingdom is offered to the
most unlikely people, despite all the objections that those who
regard themselves as likely can bring. And the more unlikely
they are, it seems, the more joyfully they receive the Kingdom.

He entered Jericho and was going through the town when
a man whose name was Zacchaeus made his appearance;

he was one of the senior tax collectors and a wealthy man. He was anxious to see what kind of man Jesus was, but he was too short and could not see him for the crowd; so he ran ahead and climbed a sycamore tree to catch a glimpse of Jesus who was to pass that way. When Jesus reached the spot he looked up and spoke to him: 'Zacchaeus, come down. Hurry, because I must stay at your house today.' And he hurried down and welcomed him joyfully. They all complained when they saw what was happening. 'He has gone to stay at a sinner's house' they said. But Zacchaeus stood his ground and said to the Lord, 'Look, sir, I am going to give half my property to the poor, and if I have cheated anybody, I will pay him back four times the amount'. And Jesus said to him, 'Today salvation has come to this house, because this man too is a son of Abraham; for the Son of Man has come to seek out and save what was lost'.

(Luke 19:1–10)

Zacchaeus was repulsive. A collaborator who exploited his own people, he deserves comparison with the worst kind of Mafia godfather. The scale of abuse of the farming-out of the right to collect taxes (and the power that gave to people near the top of the tax-collecting hierarchy over both the taxpayers and the lesser echelons of tax-collectors) were as notorious as they were resented. Anyone further removed from the poor blind man whose healing immediately precedes this story is hard to imagine.

And that, of course, is the point St Luke is making. The Kingdom is lived out in the restoration of the sight (itself a symbolic kind of healing) to the faithful poor; but, incredibly and infuriatingly, it is offered on the same (or actually better) terms to this revolting creep, Zacchaeus. No wonder 'they all complained'. According to their lights, they had much to complain about.

We are back with gratuity. Unlike most of those whom he healed, Jesus directly approaches Zacchaeus, hitherto a curious but uncommitted bystander. More, he reveals to him his human need: a meal and a bed for the night. He thus puts Zacchaeus in a privileged, even honoured, position. Whether prophet, miracle worker, healer or something much more, to

106

entertain Jesus at that point in his ministry, was to publicly associate oneself with a train of events of profound significance for all the Jewish people. Jesus offers that association to, of all people, Zacchaeus.

To a greater or lesser degree, Zacchaeus must have been conscious of the privilege that was being bestowed on him. It would be surprising, surely, if he did not immediately see the irony of this situation. Jesus, the scourge of the Pharisees and their institutionalization of God's love, throws himself on the mercy of someone whose lack of compassion for his victims was a byword. Perhaps he grasped, as supposedly secularized people sometimes do with a clarity of insight that shames us professionally religious, the enormity of what Jesus was doing.

Certainly he would have heard the tittle-tattle. 'Fancy Jesus going to spend the night with a man like *that*. . . .' Jesus would have heard it too. And maybe it was precisely the malicious gossip, the stock-in-trade of those who are finally proof against the gratuity of the Kingdom, that created a bond between them. Jesus was risking his reputation; Zacchaeus would never again be able to assert his authority in his own crooked circle.

Instead of regret or resentment, that brings joy. He is freed from a continuous assault on his deepest integrity as a person. The Law's demands of restitution to the victims of injustice (specifically *callous* injustice) and of almsgiving pose no problems now. What the day before would have seemed idiotic, unnecessary and psychologically impossible, is now done spontaneously and cheerfully. No wonder Jesus remarks that wholeness, integrity has come to this house – a double entendre for those able to see that it is Zacchaeus' reaction to Jesus, the free giver of integrity, that makes the rediscovery of integrity possible. Further gall for the small-minded and the legalistic! How could anyone talk of salvation, the rediscovery of integrity, in the same breath as a notorious sinner like Zacchaeus? If *that* was the Kingdom of Heaven that this Jesus was proclaiming . . . well, you know a man by the company he keeps, don't you?

Start this exercise by trying to recapture Zacchaeus' joy. For that is the key to the whole passage. So often we think of transformation as a painful, sorrowful business, an endless struggle against impossible odds. Much modern psycho-therapy, especially that derived from Jung or Adler, encourages us in that expectation. It is right, too. Transformation often involves a great deal of psychic pain. All the more reason, then, to enter the joy of a transformation that seems to have been untouched by pain, at least at the most creative moment.

¶Start by being Zacchaeus, at the moment Jesus spots him and walks over to the sycamore tree. Listen to what he says.... How do you react? ... Take Jesus home.... Receive him.... Introduce your family.... See that his feet are washed, that he's given sandals to wear.... Sit him down.... How do you feel as he sits in your living room? ... What do you talk about? ... What does Jesus do or say or be that touches something in you that sets you free? ... How does that moment feel? Stay with it as long as you can....

Now we turn that exercise on its head. Who are the Zacchaeuses of your world? The multi-national corporation executives who show a callous disregard for the effects of their activities on the poor of the world? The arms salesmen? The invisible purveyors of political pressure that serve special (usually moneyed) interests? The property speculators? The Stock Exchange operators who make a fat living from inside information? The international financiers who impose harsh conditions on their clients? ... I want you to identify your personal Zacchaeus-equivalents. Take them literally by the hand (they will find that almost as strange as you do!) and repeat the first exercise – only this time it is they who are in the sycamore tree.... Watch them being surprised by joy; and I want you to watch yourself being surprised by their joy.

We must now turn to a familiar objection. 'Zacchaeus may have been transformed, but the extortion racket of which he was latterly a leader continued. If the Kingdom is not about delivering the poor from the clutches of the whole system, then either it isn't the Kingdom of God – or it isn't a Kingdom worth having.' In the same vein some will argue that it is one thing to hold out the possibilities of transformation for individual managers of exploitative systems in our own world: it is quite another to change the systems that they manage. Quite. But we have to be clear that throughout the Old Testament and the New, the Kingdom changes systems by changing people. In the Old Testament the hope of shalom was based on the Covenant love between Yahweh and his people. In the New Testament, even the cosmic revolution envisioned by St John is grounded in individuals and communities being 'in Christ'. To repeat a constant theme of this book, the Kingdom is about transformation: and transformation has to be an individual process, though, as we shall see, it is one that needs to be nourished and sustained in community.

¶The last part of our exercise is now clear. Go back to your Zacchaeus-equivalent and be with her as she returns to her 'normal' activity. Watch her as she goes to the office or Capitol Hill or Parliament or Wall Street. Whom does she meet? . . . What does she say? . . . What account does she give of what she has experienced? . . . How is that received? . . . You are merely an observer; do not try to manipulate. She is a real person, not a marionette. As well as observing, however, stand alongside her. Feel the hostility . . . the ridicule . . . the questioning of professional competence . . . the rejection. . . . And offer it quietly and hopefully to God.

The Kingdom rejected

Zacchaeus was a wealthy man who was able to receive the gratuity of the Kingdom because, we have supposed, it set him free from something that assaulted his integrity. We turn now to the reverse case: a rich man who was unable to see the Kingdom around him because he was unwilling to make the leap of courageous trust which is the starting point of the Kingdom.

A member of one of the leading families put this question to him, 'Good Master, what have I to do to inherit eternal life?' Jesus said to him, 'Why do you call me good? No one is good but God alone. You know the commandments: You must not commit adultery; You must not kill; You must not steal; You must not bring false witness; Honour your father and mother.' He replied, 'I have kept all these from my earliest days till now.' And when Jesus heard this he said, 'There is still one thing you lack. Sell all that you own and distribute the money to the poor, and you will have treasure in heaven; then come, follow me.' But when he heard this he was filled with sadness, for he was very rich.

Jesus looked at him and said, 'How hard it is for those who have riches to make their way into the kingdom of God! Yes, it is easier for a camel to pass through the eye of a needle than for a rich man to enter the kingdom of God.' 'In that case' said the listeners 'who can be saved?' 'Things that are impossible for men' he replied 'are possible for God.'

(Luke 18:18–27)

Notice first that in reply to the rich aristocrat's original question, Jesus summarizes that part of the Law that has to do with social relations. By contrast with his earlier reply to the same question from a lawyer (at Luke 10:25–8), he says nothing about love of God. It is hard not to see here a depth of irony, which is already hinted at in Jesus' deflection of the aristocrat's unctuous opening. Here was a young man up to his eye-balls in 'the system' – religious, economic, political. He owed his position to the very relationships and regulations that Jesus was constantly attacking. And he was proud of his scrupulous observance of the Law! Nothing could so incarnate the bankruptcy of contemporary religion. . . . And yet Jesus takes him seriously, as he took Zacchaeus – even though under Jesus' gentle scrutiny he still does not perceive the falseness of his position. Jesus' insistence on the gratuity of the Kingdom, even for the rich and powerful, draws him to make an explicit challenge.

It is, of course, a challenge that the rich young man cannot meet. He cannot meet it because it threatens his whole milieu, his whole understanding of himself, society and God. It turns his world, with its traditional (and Old-Testament-validated) reverence for the rich as blessed by God, upside down and inside out. He would have to disown every benchmark by

which he judged – and understood – himself, and throw in
his lot with a suspicious character whom his family regarded
as subversive or mad or both. No wonder he prefers the
security of his legalistic understanding of the Law: that
preserves his status – and, it seems, his wealth.

The security that is challenged, then, is not just the security
of wealth (though Jesus constantly warns his disciples against
the dangers of wealth). It is the security of a world view that
allows to go unacknowledged, and therefore unchanged, a
whole network of relationships and power-distributions that
cocoon the rich and powerful from the shock of the Kingdom.

This is not to deny the genuineness of the enquiry of the
rich young man. Of course he wants assurance of eternal life.
But he wants it within a framework that will assure him that
nothing much will have to change. Unlike the Phoenix in
D.H. Lawrence's poem of that name, he is not ready to be
'burnt, burnt down to hot and flocculent ash'. So he could
'never really change'.

The people round found his condition and Jesus' diagnosis
of it puzzling and worrying. If not them, the rich and
powerful, then who . . . ? they ask. Unlike romantics of the
Left today, Jesus does not say, 'Why, the poor and powerless,
of course . . .' That would be to betray the radicality of the
Kingdom. The wholeness of salvation does not belong to one
class or condition: it is a gift of God, as it always was. No one
can earn or win that gift; it is given graciously, gratuitously to
those who seek it.

And that is the final condemnation of the rich young man.
It is an open question whether he is in earnest – even within
the limits of his present understanding of his position. Clearly
he is unprepared to take any risk; in that way, he is both a
far sorrier and far less noble character than Zacchaeus.
Unwilling to make any move that may jeopardize his position,
he cuts himself off from the one thing he says he is looking
for. There is no sadder plight. For it is irredeemable.

We may feel a long way, socially and psychically, from
the rich young aristocrat. Most of us are neither rich nor
aristocratic. We should see him, however, as a symbol – a
symbol of those parts of us and our communities that are
looking for the Kingdom on the cheap, a Kingdom without
serious threat to the *status quo*, a Kingdom that leaves things

pretty much as they are in Church and State as well as in our own inner lives. How hard it is for that part of us to enter the Kingdom of God. How desperately we want to cling on to those bits of our world that affirm us, that give us status and self-understanding. 'It won't matter if . . .'

¶For the first exercise on this passage, try identifying for yourself and your community (and interpret that as you will) how the Kingdom threatens the *status quo*. What, for you, is the cost of the Kingdom? . . . What world-views, perceptions, attitudes, assumptions are challenged by it? . . . What loss of understanding, of moral and intellectual security? . . . And what physical security? . . . This is a hard exercise, and one that you will perhaps find yourself returning to again and again. For only as much will come clear to us as we can handle at the time. Rather like an antibiotic, the truth of the cost of the Kingdom can enter the bloodstream only gradually.

The second part of the exercise, the meditative rather than the analytical, is simply to lay that cost before God. Do not fight great inner battles to force yourself to pay the costs you have identified in the first part of the exercise. No good and possibly much damage will come of that. Rather, lay it gently and lovingly before God and quietly acknowledge its reality. Then leave it to him. As and when he requires you to pay the costs you have identified, he will draw you gently forward and sustain you as you let go . . . and you will find that the terror you expected is replaced by a growing conviction of his companionship.

The third part of the exercise is similar to the exercise on Zacchaeus. Identify one 'rich young aristocrat' in local or national life – a person, that is to say, in a position of influence or power who would find the gratuity of the Kingdom too shocking and too costly; for whom, in other words, 'letting go' is even more difficult than it is for you or me. Recognizing that we have the same problem – and in this sense in solidarity with him or her – stand alongside him/her before Christ, and simply acknowledge the difficulty. . . .

We have seen the Kingdom offered, described, lived out, accepted and rejected, and we have tried to use that drama as meditative material for prayer at many levels – from the individual to the cosmic. A sub-theme throughout this exploration has been that the gratuity of the Kingdom involves suffering. It brings rejection and contempt to those who proclaim and live it; and it brings pain and anguish to those who, glimpsing it, want to reach out to it and make it their own.

It is time now to go more deeply into this theme. For it is central in the biblical record; it is central in the history of the Church; and it is central in the life of communities to-day that look for the coming of the Kingdom. There is always a temptation, perhaps felt particularly keenly by those exposed to a romantic version of liberation theology, to neglect or minimize the costliness of the Kingdom. It seems to be roughly true that the more superficially secular is the notion of the Kingdom, the greater is that temptation. After all, the social engineer usually operates by consensus; and consensus is only possible by a strategy of cost minimization. At the other, deeper, end of the spectrum, however, where the Kingdom is conceived as a great cosmic triumph of the force of love over the power of evil, the suffering of self-offering is literally inevitable. For that is the only *kind* of triumph that does not reinforce the power of evil and thus defeat its own objective.

In this exercise, then, we have to go as near the heart of that cosmic struggle as we feel able to penetrate. That means going as close to the seat of the pain that wins the struggle as we dare.

The passers-by jeered at him; they shook their heads and said, 'Aha! So you would destroy the Temple and rebuild it in three days! Then save yourself: come down from the cross!' The chief priests and the scribes mocked him among themselves in the same way. 'He saved others,' they said 'he cannot save himself. Let the Christ, the king of Israel, come down from the cross now, for us to see it and believe.' Even those who were crucified with him taunted him.

When the sixth hour came there was darkness over the whole land until the ninth hour. And at the ninth hour

Jesus cried out in a loud voice, 'Eloi, Eloi, lama sabach-
thani?' which means, 'My God, my God, why have you
deserted me?' When some of those who stood by heard this,
they said, 'Listen, he is calling on Elijah'. Someone ran
and soaked a sponge in vinegar and, putting it on a reed,
gave it him to drink saying, 'Wait and see if Elijah will
come to take him down'. But Jesus gave a loud cry and
breathed his last.

(Mark 15:29–37)

This account of the crucifixion has two clear references to
Psalm 22. The mocking is almost a direct quotation:

> They toss their heads and sneer,
> 'He relied on Yahweh, let Yahweh save him!
> If Yahweh is his friend, let Him rescue him.'

(Psalm 22:7–8)

Similarly, Jesus' words reported here comprise the first line
of the Psalm, often used contemporarily as a title:

> My God, my God why have you deserted me?
> How far from saving me, the words I groan!
> I call all day, my God, but you never answer,
> all night long I call and cannot rest.

(Psalm 22:1–2)

There is a third reference to this Psalm in two other accounts
of the crucifixion. Both Matthew and John record the division
of Christ's clothes.

> . . . they glare at me, gloating:
> they divide my garments among them
> and cast lots for my clothes.

(Psalm 22:17–18)

It is beyond our purposes to enter the academic debate about
how far Psalm 22 influenced the Gospel narratives: what is
clear is that for Christ himself the Psalm vividly portrayed
the consciousness of intense suffering, raised to a higher power
by the sense of being spurned, in his most acute need, by
God the Father.

114

Do not stand aside; trouble is near,
I have no one to help me!

(Psalm 22:11)

The nadir is here. Rejected by the religious establishment throughout his ministry, he has been rejected by the people he thought he had come to bring with him into the Kingdom. Having hailed him as the one to set them free only days before, they lift not a finger to help him; they even join in the jeering. They will not accept the quality of love he offers; and they dismiss the lover with the love.

The one solace, the one psychic prop remaining, is the knowledge that in doing the will of the Father he is assured of the presence, perhaps even the mighty liberating presence, of the Father who will deliver him from the cross – perhaps physically, but certainly morally and inwardly.

Rescue my soul from the sword,
my dear life from the paw of the dog,
save me from the lion's mouth,
my poor soul from the wild bulls' horns!

(Psalm 22:20–1)

Nothing happens. Nothing. . . . The physical pain grows worse as death approaches. The mocking and gloating continue. The disciples are scattered. The women watch in silence from a distance. Defeat is absolute. The Kingdom has failed before it even began.

And there we face the ultimate paradox. For Psalm 22 ends with a shout of praise and glory to Yahweh *because the Kingdom lives.*

. . . you who fear Yahweh, praise him!
Entire race of Jacob, glorify him!
Entire race of Israel, revere him!
For he has not despised
or disdained the poor man in his poverty, . . .
The poor will receive as much as they want to eat. . . .
The whole earth, from end to end, will remember and come
    back to Yahweh. . . .
For Yahweh reigns, the ruler of nations!
Before him all the prosperous of the earth will bow
    down, . . .

(Psalm 22:23–4, 26–9)

115

At the moment of total defeat, the politics of the Magnificat, in strikingly similar language, are reaffirmed. Because love has finally yielded every last vestige of self-protection – even the assurance of Yahweh's deliverance – the Kingdom of God, with its message of hope for the poor and judgement for the rich, can be offered afresh. This is mystery: many say it is nonsense. We trust – often with desperate, even failing, courage – that Christ's final self-giving turns the tide in the cosmic struggle and therefore makes it possible to ally one's forces, however puny, with those that will bring the Kingdom. 'For Yahweh reigns . . . !'

We may never be called to share the vortex of suffering that the cross represents and symbolizes. There is something unique about Christ's death; and it is not for us to seek to replicate it. There are, however, thousands of 'ordinary' people who find themselves, often to their surprise, taking part in the same drama. Their role is not representational, in the sense that Christian doctrine sees Christ's death as representing the whole of humanity, but it is re-presentational in the sense that it brings to life the capacity of suffering love to overthrow and transform the forces of evil. Think of the stories in chapter 4 and your own equivalents.

It goes deeper than that. The Franciscan community in El Salvador is living it out, incarnating it. That is one level of reality, the level of actuality. But there is another level of reality, the level of spirituality. Those of us who are not called to live out the struggle for the Kingdom re-presentationally are called to live it out psychically and spiritually. That is, we are called to lend our 'soul-force', our deepest psychic energies to the creative role of suffering love.

¶Let's start by recalling our own moments of dereliction, of utter defeat. Most of us sooner or later go through a period when, having tried to be constructive and liberating in our own environment, we find ourselves rejected, often by close friends or those on whose side we thought we were fighting. That rejection is made worse by the fact that God suddenly seems far off. He has abandoned us in the mire. It is a hard time . . . Recall it; dwell on it. . . .

You will probably be aware of elements in the experience that point to negative features in your own personality. 'If

only I hadn't been so proud (or busy or angry or careless
. . .) it need never have happened . . .' Leave those to one
side; this is not the time to learn from them. Rather see that
experience, especially the distance of God, as a privileged
glimpse into the heart of Christ at the moment of dereliction.
In as much as we can have solidarity with Christ at that
point, so much we enter the mystery of the self-giving suffering
that calls forward the Kingdom. . . . Offer it quietly . . .
humbly, for his suffering was of a different order to ours. And
his innocence was absolute.

Now offer those times of dereliction, of complete defeat and
abandonment, as they are suffered by others in the struggle for
the Kingdom. You may or may not know people personally; I
hope you will have been collecting stories since you read
chapter 4 and may therefore be well-armed! Remember those
people at times when they know the totality of failure. For
that is the creative moment; that is the moment when Yahweh
reigns. For it is the moment of our powerlessness, our release
of our ultimate securities, even of faith itself. Love that
endures that existential annihilation releases cosmic forces
that will bring the Kingdom.

Finally, as a counterpoint to the last two rather taxing
exercises, we change gear to complete fantasy. I want you to
be a witness at the crucifixion. You know the conventional
scene well enough. . . . Recreate it. . . . Then over the brow
of the hill comes a great mob of poor, half-starving, diseased
and crippled men, women and children. Dozens of them.
Hundreds. . . . And they are all smiling and laughing and
shouting. . . . They gather at the foot of the cross and cheer
Jesus. They cheer and cheer, as if a winning goal had just
been scored in a cup-tie. He tries to say something to them,
but in the effort he dies. Now they go mad, flinging their hats
in the air, embracing each other. They rip the cross out of
the ground, gently remove the body and carry it shoulder
high, still celebrating with every ounce of their strength. . . .
I want you to mingle with that crowd. . . . Ask them why
they are behaving like this. . . . Ask them what Jesus was
trying to say. . . . If you feel like it, join in. . . .

117

The Kingdom reoffered

Some people will find the last exercise difficult – at many levels. 'You are cheating', they will say, 'it is the resurrection that is the occasion for joy, not the crucifixion.' They are right: but they are only half right. For it is the quality of love that the cross demonstrates that makes the resurrection the natural – one might almost say inevitable – sequel. We are back to our original motif. Like Yahweh in the Old Testament, Jesus offers a quality of love to the people that is the first fruit of the Kingdom. Like Yahweh, he finds his offer spurned. In a final demonstration of the transformative power of the love he has been offering, he experiences the full horror of rejection, pain and failure. The Jews, despite some nervous misgivings, assume that is that. So, in a different key, do the disciples.

But God does not let go. He is not prepared to abandon the Kingdom – especially now that an event of cosmic significance has happened at Golgotha. Within three days God the Son is back – again proclaiming the Kingdom. And again being ignored.

Having risen in the morning on the first day of the week, he appeared first to Mary of Magdala from whom he had cast out seven devils. She then went to those who had been his companions, and who were mourning and in tears, and told them. But they did not believe her when they heard her say that he was alive and that she had seen him.

After this, he showed himself under another form to two of them as they were on their way into the country. These went back and told the others, who did not believe them either.

Lastly, he showed himself to the Eleven themselves while they were at table. He reproached them for their incredulity and obstinacy, because they had refused to believe those who had seen him after he had risen. And he said to them, 'Go out to the whole world; proclaim the Good News to all creation. He who believes and is baptised will be saved; he who does not believe will be condemned.'

(Mark 16:9–16)

The grief and despair of the disciples was such that they had concluded that Yahweh had given up. Perhaps they had taken Psalm 22 – or the first half of it – at face value. Whatever they now thought of the meaning of Jesus' ministry, they were clear that the wild adventure of the last two years was over. No surprise, then, that they did not know him.

No surprise either that Jesus finds their incredulity reproachful. After all he had taught them of the quality of love – and then they just give up in despair! He must have wondered whether they had learnt anything from his two years with them; and yet it was to these people, hopeless and faithless as they were, that he was to entrust the final acting out of the offer of transforming love.

We need to be clear, however, that the Great Commission as it is sometimes called – 'Go out among all nations . . .' – is deeply rooted in the political realities of Israel. The good news is about Yahweh's deliverance from oppression, from exploitation and aggression. For the reference is unmistakably to Isaiah 52, a poem on the liberation of Jerusalem:

> Shake off your dust; to your feet,
> captive Jerusalem!
> Free your neck from its fetters,
> captive daughter of Zion.

(Isaiah 52:2)

What is remarkable about this poem – and Jesus' use of it – is the prose insertion that follows immediately after that verse. It is a paragraph full of emphasis, almost as though the editor of Deutero-Isaiah was underlining something that he thought his readers might otherwise miss – or misunderstand.

Yes, Yahweh says this: You were sold for nothing and you will be redeemed without money. Yes, Yahweh says this: Once my people went to Egypt to settle there, then Assyria bitterly oppressed them. . . . – it is Yahweh who speaks – all day long my name is constantly blasphemed. My people will therefore know my name: that day they will understand that it is I who say, 'I am here'.

(Isaiah 52:3–6)

The poem then resumes with the verse banalized by repetition:

How beautiful on the mountains
are the feet of one who brings good news,
who heralds peace, brings happiness,
proclaims salvation,
and tells Zion,
'Your God is King'.

(Isaiah 52:7)

Notice, then, how political liberation, economic justice and international harmony are held together with a wholeness and wholesomeness that stems from the acknowledgement of the Kingdom of Yahweh.

This is the good news the disciples are to proclaim. The love of God Father and Son will show itself in peace and prosperity, but only when 'Zion' hears, in the deepest Johannine sense, that God reigns. Christ is, however, radically innovative. The good news is no longer just for Zion, for Israel. It is for all creation. Leave aside the question of whether that is a later, post-Pauline, memory: the understanding of the early Church as reflected in all four Gospels is that the good news of social and individual wholeness is cosmic in its extent.

Proclamation of the Kingdom is now to be universal. For the Kingdom, and the love affair on which it depends, is for the whole of human society. Indeed it is for everything that ever was or ever will be. Only so can it become real. Peace, justice, harmony, prosperity are not divisible. Interdependence has become a political truism in the last ten years. The older wisdom of the resurrection narrative, however, made the Kingdom universal, not because that is the only way it will work, but because God's love for his creation knows no racial or territorial bounds. Those who can accept it will grow into a wholeness and fullness that looks forward to the final triumph: those who follow the tradition of .srael and her leaders by rejecting it condemn themselves to an enduring impoverishment.

¶For meditation, perhaps you would like to take one of the following from chapter 4: the young South African soldier in Namibia; the refugees in El Salvador; the drop-out society among whom Cathy lived for a while or the peasants among whom Flora works. Alternatively you might like to identify a group among whom you live or work, not necessarily under-privileged or oppressed. . . . Then tell them in non-technical, non-churchy language what is the good news for them – for them as they are, in their particular situation, . . . and what do you want them to do about it?

If you find this very hard, you are at least in good company! Maybe a better way is to imagine the group you have selected meeting the risen Christ along with the eleven disciples. Let Christ talk to them; and let them talk to Christ. . . . Give it time. . . . You may well be surprised by the conversation.

If it still seems hard, do not imagine you are a failure or deficient in some way. Go back to the eleven and watch them throughout this scene. . . . And then listen to what they say when Christ disappears. . . . What do they think Christ meant? . . . What does it mean for them?

It might be appropriate to end the exercise with a grateful acknowledgement of the lovingness of God. . . . The news he wants us to hear is *good*. Thank him for that.

The Kingdom enabled

The cosmic transformation to which the resurrection points depends crucially on the proclamation of Kingdom-love by those, supposedly 'The Church', who have glimpsed its poten-tial. What a task!

It is a task so beyond us that we need help. The new task brings new resources – or at least powerful reassurance of the effective presence of resources that the Old Testament knows something of, albeit in an unsystematic and even vague way. Now the Holy Spirit is given as a permanent guarantee of energy and enabling power. The fear that is a constant reac-tion to God's invitation in the Old Testament (and even in the Gospels) is to be met by a new Spirit of boldness and heedlessness of personal safety. Notice for example the repetition of derivatives of 'bold' in our final reading.

'And now, Lord, take note of their threats and help your servants to proclaim your message with all boldness, by stretching out your hand to heal and to work miracles and marvels through the name of your holy servant Jesus.' As they prayed, the house where they were assembled rocked; they were all filled with the Holy Spirit and began to proclaim the word of God boldly.

The whole group of believers was united, heart and soul; no one claimed for his own use anything that he had, as everything they owned was held in common.

The apostles continued to testify to the resurrection of the Lord Jesus with great power, and they were all given great respect.

None of their members was ever in want, as all those who owned land or houses would sell them, and bring the money from them, to present it to the apostles; it was then distributed to any members who might be in need.

(Acts 4:29–35)

The context is that, having healed a cripple, Peter and John are hauled before the Sanhedrin. The members of that august body, something akin to a bishops' conference, do not know how to cope with the new situation. Having thought that by getting rid of Jesus, the problems he posed would go away, they find the very reverse. By invoking his name, 'uneducated laymen' are performing miraculous cures, and the people, the ordinary men and women in the street, who were ready to join in the mockery of Jesus at Golgotha, are now in an ugly mood. They are beginning to suspect that their leaders have made a grave mistake: and Peter and John are tactless enough to go on spelling it out in explicit detail. . . . 'Christ the Nazarene, the one you crucified . . . the stone rejected by you the builders . . .' The leaders try to persuade Peter and John to keep quiet, but they, with courage underwritten by the Spirit, simply tell them that if it is a matter of obeying men or God, they will obey God. They return to the believing community who pray to God, in the words of the passage above, for courage to proclaim 'your message'.

Luke, then, by skilful juxtaposition of his source material, spells out what that 'message', the 'good news', comprises. It is healing and working 'miracles and marvels'. It is unity and harmony in the community. It is the willing renunciation of private property. It is joyful sharing. And it is the proclamation of the fact that Christ 'whom you killed' is, in fact, alive and present among the believing community.

In our terminology, these are all symbols of the transformation that the love of God calls out, and which, we now say, the Spirit enables. We must never drive a wedge between those two parts of God's action — his evocative love and the enablement of the Spirit. Certainly the characteristics of the Spirit sometimes *look* quite different from the tender, compassionate, patient love of God. The Spirit is wind and fire — both ruthless, indiscriminate and destructive. He makes the house rock in this passage. He bestows the strange and unnerving gift of 'tongues', so that bystanders think the apostles have been drinking too much new wine, itself an interesting comment on the disorderliness of the Spirit. He is the source of boldness, of a reckless courage. He is wild, passionate, uncareful.

From that it does not follow, however, that he is care*less*. He is the passionate, spirited, disturbing side of God's love. There is much classical Christian doctrine about the Trinity which emphasizes that it is the quality of love that holds together the Three in one, rather as lovers experience a psychic unity in the depth of their shared love. Classical doctrine may or may not help us pray for the Kingdom: I mention it only to emphasize the continuity between the love of Yahweh and the work of the Spirit.

For both are transformative. Both evoke and enable a change in human behaviour, which itself both points to and constitutes the coming of the Kingdom. Forgive a homely parable. I have just been up the track at the back of the cottage. Yesterday was one of those warm, damp winter days when the sodden leaves form a soggy sponge, squelching under one's boots. After a few degrees of frost, those sodden, meaningless leaves have each become radiant with beauty. Their edges and spines sparkling with hoar-frost, they flash in the sun reflecting indigo, gold and purest white. Each is differentiated from the other, and each adds its own appeal to the delight of a frosty morning. A drop in temperature of a few degrees has left everything where it was; but it has changed it from a sloshy mess to a source of wonder. . . . Such is the work of the Spirit.

123

¶As an exercise, start with the apostles and the believing community, as they meet, after the ordeal of Peter and John before the Sanhedrin, to share in prayer to the Father. Just *be* there . . . listen . . . watch . . . be alert to the presence of the Spirit among them. . . . Prayers are over. How do they relate to each other? . . . What is the atmosphere like? . . .

Now, think of any community you have visited or belonged to where transformation was actually happening: where people were being healed, spiritually or physically; where envy, greed, possessiveness were in retreat; where relationships were healthy, sensitive and robust; where you could feel a joyfulness that you could intuit had something to do with the fact of the resurrection. . . . A tall order? Of course. But you will be unfortunate never to have come into contact with any community where these features are present, even if only in embryo. If you have never done so, this might be a good time to pray that you will be. If, as I expect, you do know such a place, warts and all, thank God for the work of the Spirit there . . . and then, as it were, let it grow . . . let that community grow inwards, as it deepens its common life in response to the enabling energy of the Spirit, but let it also grow outwards . . . don't worry about the mechanics of growth . . . pray that what is special about it may extend, be shared, be taken over by others . . . like yeast expanding a lump of dough, see it gradually rise till it fills the whole space – of your locality, your region, your country, the world . . . let the Spirit *in* . . .

Finally, think of your own parable of transformation, like, but better than, mine above about the leaves. Your everyday life is littered with them. That might surprise you, but I think you will find it is true. . . . Then take any institution or power group or set of demonic forces that seem the opposite of the Kingdom and offer them to God in the light of your parable . . . you will find that you are praying with the Spirit . . . and you are praying for the transformation of the Kingdom.

8

Prayer and the worshipping community

Many of the exercises that were introduced in chapters 5, 6 and 7 lend themselves naturally to work in groups. This is particularly true of the analytical or descriptive parts of the exercises, but even the fantasies can be done together. For just as some people can think analytically more naturally than others, so some have greater imaginative power. In the more inward, meditative phases, most people find silence the biggest help: but a shared silence can be supportive. I know people much experienced in prayer who find their prayer comes alive in a silence shared by others much more readily than it does in solitude.

We should not be surprised, then, to find the kind of prayer we have been exploring 'spilling over' into the more formal parts of the church's liturgical life. Like over-active yeast in a baking tin of dough, it will spill over the edges and creep over the kitchen table. Like such excess, however, it needs controlling, marshalling and putting to good use. Otherwise it will be wasted, and perhaps even harmful.

It hardly needs saying that formal liturgy is not the same animal as the prayer of informal, closely-bonded groups of people who might share in some of the explorations of the last three chapters. By its very nature, formal liturgy is more impersonal, stylized, and abstract. That is what makes it 'common', available to people of widely different backgrounds and expectations. Too often, however, that necessary degree of stylization is allowed to dominate liturgical expression. The result is that the people, whose 'work' the liturgy is supposed to be, find it hard, even impossible, to 'enter' the prayers in a way that brings the whole drama alive for them – or, one may safely assume, for God. Too many services are boring, unimaginative, dead and deadening. They are not likely to be

the vehicles by which God's love for his people is proclaimed –
'what I want is love . . .' – or by which the people are made
aware of the transforming possibilities of that love. In that
case, they are more likely to be obstacles to the Kingdom
than heralds of it.

It is easy, and cheap, to make such general condemnations.
Let me emphasize at once, therefore, that I have no slick
solutions; that I recognize that making liturgy live is one of
the most difficult and problem-ridden areas of the Church's
life (and in that I include every mainline tradition); and that
what follows is no more than a tiny drop in a large bucket,
which will have to be filled by more creative brains than
mine.

Further, we have already seen some of the dangers. I have
attended specially prepared 'justice' or 'aid' liturgies that
manage to embrace most of them – engendering (but not
dealing with) guilt, degenerating into propaganda or news-
casting services, indulging in 'heavy' teaching as though the
glory of God depended upon his people gaining A level passes
in international politics. Some ministers are so anxious to
make explicit their commitment to the poor, that the liturgy
begins to sound like an ideological closed shop. The Earl of
Stockton (formerly Harold Macmillan, British Prime Minister
1957 to 1963) complained to a member of the Church of
England synod that he was finding going to his village church
an increasingly puzzling experience: 'Every Sunday seems to
be Guerrilla Sunday.' Nevertheless I have every sympathy
with his vicar. Tied to a liturgy that takes neither Kingdom
nor justice nor peace too seriously, over-reaction is
understandable.

Understandable but not finally creative. How do we, then,
bring the liturgy alive to the good news of the coming of the
Kingdom without falling into any of these traps? Without any
pretence that they contain a comprehensive solution, I offer
comments on five themes: situation, stories, symbols, silence,
and sacrament.

Situation

Liturgy does not – or at any rate should not – happen in a vacuum. I suspect that one reason why my own tradition, perhaps more than that of the 'gathered' Churches on the one hand and the Roman Catholic on the other, finds liturgy so hard to bring alive is precisely that it is cut off from life. For many people, an hour in church on Sunday is exactly that – an hour in church on Sunday. It is not much different from an annual visit to the dentist or a monthly visit to the in-laws; that is to say it is a routine that has its own specific agenda and its own rationale, but neither reationale nor agenda relate livingly to the events of the community in which the liturgy is performed.

This can give rise to some astonishing incongruities which would be comic if they were not so tragic. We have all experienced them. The day after the first serious public disorder in the capital since independence in 1964, an Anglican congregation in Lusaka, Zambia, prayed for peace in Northern Ireland. When the consciences of many people in the West were being moved by the first film reports of the Ethiopian famine of 1983–5, harvest festival services gave thanks for the creation of additional unwanted surpluses of grain in Europe and America. . . .

This takes us back to one of our earlier exercises. We need to ask, surely, where are the signs of the Kingdom *in our own community?* Where are the values of the Kingdom being lived out – not just talked about or written about? . . . We find that a difficult and even threatening question. Bishop Stephen Verney recounts how he set himself the task of sitting down with every church council in the diocese and asking each one: 'What is God doing *here* and *now?*' Some people told him it was an improper, even indecent, question. 'You can't expect God to be *here* – not *now* . . .' That seldom lasted. 'Slowly, after time for reflection, people began to share amazing insights of grace at work in individuals, groups, whole communities. . . . It was clear that for many it was the first time they had thought of it in that way . . . and what a joyful discovery it was for them! Perhaps, after all, God was alive and living amongst them.'

My hunch is that Stephen Verney's experience is almost

universal: that people do not look for the Kingdom to break
in around them, because they do not expect to find anything
if they do. And yet when they do look, they are astonished
and delighted at what they discover.

This is not to say that if you go to Wigan or Wichita, you
will find the Beatitudes fulfilled in the High Street. The
process is more subtle, more ambiguous, more provisional: it
needs discernment and the eye of faith to see where God is
working. And it is that which makes it awkward to incorporate into the worshipping life of the community. We are
often dealing with the first faint signs of spring; rarely with
the luscious leafiness of high summer. Nonetheless, once we
learn to look in the expectation of finding at least some signs
of life, we have something that is naturally taken up in
worship in two ways.

First, it is something *worth* or *worthy* that makes wor(th)ship
a rooted experience. Strangers are being welcomed; communities are being healed; the homeless are being housed; mour-
ners are being comforted: small in themselves as these acts
may be, they are pointers to the Kingdom in the situation of
this community at this time, and as such are worth praising
God for. From thanksgiving and praise stems prayer for their
nourishment and extension – and, as we shall consider at
greater length in the last chapter, a deepening commitment
to them.

Second, in so far as the congregation is involved in living
out those pointers to the Kingdom, worship becomes part of
the process by which they are sustained. If it can be brought
alive by rising from and returning to the situation of the
worshipping community, liturgy can be a rich source of
nourishment. Because the love of God in Christ is represented in story, song and sacrament, the people of God
can be nourished in that love. This is far removed from the
diet of guilt, burden and obligation that I fear many church-
goers derive from their church-going. It is the difference
between a liturgy that enables and a liturgy that crushes.
Behind that, of course, lurks the difference between a God
who longs for his people to recognize and return his love (the
biblical God I have tried to present); and the Moloch God
who wants endless sacrifice whom most of us have put in his

place, aided and abetted in that fatal substitution by the 'worship' to which we have been subjected.

To summarize this section, liturgy has to relate to the situation-in-life of the worshipping community. That community can be encouraged to see around it, in its own place, incipient signs of the Kingdom. This recognition can be brought alive in worship in praise, thanksgiving and intercession; but it can also nourish the community, not least by assuring it of the nature of the God it serves.

Stories

This is familiar territory by now. I have tried to show in chapters 4 to 7 how 'stories' or 'myths' can bring prayer alive, by earthing our fantasies in the rich humus of the experience of others. I want to suggest now that story has a similar role to play in the life of the whole worshipping community.

This is especially true in those communities in which, for whatever reason, there is a great gulf between the life of the worshipping community and the signs of the Kingdom. This is a pathological (but common) condition since it means that the local church has distanced itself from the work of the Spirit in its own locality. As with an ambassador who discovers that his head of state is staying incognito in a *pension* down the road from the embassy, this suggests not only a breakdown of communication: it suggests a breakdown of a relationship. One way of restoring that relationship is by exposing the worshipping community to stories, in the sense I defined in chapter 4, drawn from its own secular community (where the signs of the Kingdom are apparent) and from further afield. In my experience, a church in the pathological condition I have described will more readily 'hear' the latter than the former – and will perhaps remain exceedingly resistant to the former for a long time. For the Kingdom is much more handleable 'out there' than it is 'right here'. As long as it involves 'them', 'we' will support them with our money and prayers and feel safe and secure in doing so. But if it is going to involve 'us' in standing alongside the poor, in welcoming them, in struggling for justice, well, that's different.

The transition from stories about the breaking in of the Kingdom 'out there' to what it involves, is now involving, right here is fraught with danger and difficulty. Shortly after I arrived at Christian Aid, we issued a film strip called 'Christians and Social Change'. It told the story, in a fairly low-key way, of the Church's involvement in the struggle for justice in Nicaragua, El Salvador, South Korea and the Philippines. It then changed style from technicolour to black and white; from voice over to music over; from thematic images that stayed on the screen for twenty or thirty seconds to random quick-flash images – images of poverty, degradation, pollution, squalor and conflict in Britain in the 1980s. The reaction was explosive. I was inundated with letters, telephone calls, visitors . . . how dare I sanction the production of this Communist propaganda? In every case it turned out that congregations had no difficulty with the Church standing alongside the poor 'out there'. But to suggest that that stance could not be allowed to stay 'out there' indefinitely was an outrage . . . 'And we don't want any of that theological nonsense either,' added a senior Board member.

One reason why that reaction was so angry, I believe, was precisely that we did not take sufficient trouble with *story*. The final sequence of pin-prick shots were devoid of story: we were back with the old firm of Guilt and Powerlessness. I conclude then that the transition will be made less threatening, more easily internalized if the change of focus is communicated in stories – and incarnated in people.

Although there are a number of risks here, especially in a small locality where everybody knows everything about everybody – and what they don't know they make up – the advantages of having someone identifiable tell the story usually greatly outweigh the dangers. For a person can centre prayer in a way a name or an institution cannot. That is true for an individual; and it is true for a church.

An ideal way of achieving this transition and of simultaneously guarding against a worshipping community becoming exclusively concerned with its own place is to expose the community over a period to a dialogue between a 'story-teller' from 'out there' and a 'story-teller' from 'right here'. This can bring out the parallels and contrasts between what it means to stand for the Kingdom in a safe, far-distant environment; and what it means down the road tomorrow morning. I recognize, of course, that logistically this is not an easy trick to pull off. The number and availability of ace 'story-tellers' from 'out there' is not large – though it is far larger than the international Church bureaucracy recognizes or enables. There are, however, often local substitutes who can talk from their own experience – recent immigrants or their visitors from 'home', overseas students, refugees, even visiting dignitaries, diplomats or officials.

There is a skill in using these stories in worship. A crude, insensitive, pedestrian or sycophantic 'incorporation' of them will diminish rather than enrich the worship of the community. Indeed such an approach can be comical: once, when in northern Namibia, I was surprised and amused to find myself likened, line by line, to the prophet bringing good news from a far country! The sensitive, suggestive use of biblical material alongside stories can, however, be helpful, providing always that the integrity of that material is respected and not just manipulated.

To summarize, I have suggested that story has a key role to play in putting the church in touch with what God is doing. Stories from distant lands are heard more easily than stories from the home front, but a mutual interaction of the two sources can be powerful. Care and creativity are required in incorporating them in worship, but the benefits of doing so can be surprisingly generous.

Symbols

Any public act of worship in virtually any religion uses symbols. For humans are symbol-loving animals: indeed they live by symbols. Deprived of contact with the symbol-rich knowledge of their own and the collective unconscious, they soon fall apart – as has been experimentally demonstrated. Anyone who has taken their own dream life seriously cannot but be aware of how central symbolism is to the inner life of each one of us. Symbols speak to us with all the subtlety and suggestiveness of great poetry. They do not define or encase precise propositions. They hint. They point. They nudge us along. They 'put us on to' meaning, feelings, states of consciousness. They thus call forth our own creativity, imagination and openness – precisely the faculties that enrich prayer (and precisely the faculties that much 'public prayer' actively discourages, with its emphasis on intellectualization and, at best, some kind of affective assent).

The trick then is to identify and use symbols that mobilize those faculties and relate them to the Kingdom.

As I argued that the Kingdom is all around us if only we would look expectantly for it, so I argue now that relevant, evocative symbols are around us if we would only look for them. Every culture and sub-culture throws up its own symbols, and inherits the symbols of earlier cultures, giving them new life and meaning.

It has been one of the functions of religion in most cultures to undertake this symbol-reinterpretation for the whole culture. Religion is, as it were, a symbol warehouse, where symbols are stored, regilded and re-lent to the main-stream of life. But the stock should be slowly changing. The warehouse may manufacture some of its own symbols – which is fine if its wares are well known to the public. Or it may receive symbols from the public and, as it were, incorporate them into its stock.

Some examples may help. The Christian Church has generated a host of symbols, of which the cross and its many variants are the most obvious. Others are bread and wine; light (as in candle-light); the fish-sign; the bark or ship. Some it has borrowed from pagan culture: eggs, flowers, and many of the Christmas symbols such as holly and mistletoe. In many parts of the world this 'borrowing' is proceeding apace. The Roman Catholic Bishop of Kumasi, in Ghana, for example has done much to promote the symbols of the Ashanti in his churches. The former Anglican Bishop of Kurunegala in Sri Lanka saw Buddhism as the Old Testament of his people, and the stonework of his cathedral incorporates Buddhist symbols rather than medieval gargoyles. Fr Bede Griffiths has incorporated much Hindu symbolism into the liturgy of his ashram at Shantivanam, in south India.

My contention is that we need to follow the courageous examples of such people and invent our own symbols, or borrow them from the pagan culture in which most of us live.

Some of this, is, of course, already happening. White roses have become an almost universal symbol of 'the Disappeared' in Latin America. Red roses represent and recall the modern martyrs of the Church. Chains are sometimes offered on the altar with the bread and wine as a symbol of the fact that though we are all made free in Christ, too many of our fellow men and women are still in physical or metaphorical chains. The peace movement has been an unusually prolific source of its own symbolism; significantly this is especially true of the women's peace movement. The white poppy of peace, the children's toys, variants of the original CND symbol, crossed warheads . . . some of these will find their way to the warehouse and become semi-permanent features of our symbolic landscape.

The peace movement is not untypical. The ecological movement, the feminist movement, and much 'pop' culture are constantly throwing up their own symbols – as the rash of buttons on sale on every university campus attests. We are surrounded by symbols but, lacking the courage and creativity of our friends in Ghana, Sri Lanka, India and tens of other so-called Third World countries, we turn our backs on them.

Let us be clear. It *does* take courage and creativity to adopt non-Christian, usually politically loaded, symbols, and make of them symbols that arouse the deep springs of prayerfulness in a congregation. Indeed, I doubt if it can be done effectively from 'outside' or be imposed on a congregation. Ideally it arises from its own experience, emerging from its own attempt to live the Kingdom; or, less ideally, from a real 'entering into' the kind of stories we have been considering.

I can offer only one example from my own recent experience. An ecumenical group on Merseyside, struggling in that difficult environment with the connectedness of injustice in their own place and global injustice, wanted to re-present the sense they had of being sustained by the love of God in that struggle. They took an admittedly already Christian symbol, namely bread, but reinterpreted it in an original way that said precisely what they wanted it to say. At the beginning of the liturgy they ritually made bread, mixing the named ingredients: Here is flour, given in harvest . . . Here is water, sign of our saving . . . Here is yeast, sign of our calling . . .

133

Representatives of the community kneaded the dough, symbolizing the hard work required to 'make bread'. The dough was taken away, and at the end of the liturgy, the baked bread was formally broken and shared: 'God feeds us, his people . . .'

Precious? Over-elaborate? Prissy? . . . The proof of the pudding is in how it lives on in the memory; how it evokes, nourishes prayer; how it feeds imagination and at the same time binds the community together. On those criteria I can only report as honestly as I can: it worked for me and for many more.

The question remains: can we find 'new' symbols (which may, of course, not be really new at all) that 'speak' of the Kingdom in this evocative way? And having found them, have we the guts to use them?

My hunch is that the peace movement is throwing up symbols that are 'ripe for conversion', as the estate agents put it. Indeed congregations in many parts of the United States, especially in colleges and universities, are beginning to adopt and adapt these symbols. They are becoming signs, not of membership of a particular organization or political persuasion, but of the hope of the Kingdom – and a pledge to live that hope. . . . Perhaps it is significant that there are no equivalent processes to symbolize in Christian worship the struggle of the domestic poor; and precious few to symbolize the struggle of the 600 million of the world's poor. For we are all threatened by nuclear disaster. The articulate symbol-makers are not, at least as they see it, much threatened by the poverty of the unemployed blacks, or by the near starvation of the landless of Africa and Asia.

Silence

One of the most solemn sermons I have ever heard was on the subject of joy. I find myself caught in a similar contradiction when writing about silence. Silence is not to be written or spoken about. It is to be lived, experienced, enjoyed.

Let me then say as briefly as may be that silence has a creative part to play in bringing worship in general and prayer for the Kingdom alive. Our culture does not welcome silence:

notice how many people, finding themselves alone in a house, immediately turn on a radio or television. Our public worship shares this dread of silence. 'Play something,' hisses the officiant to the organist as soon as there is a pause in the endless stream of sound.

Yet silence is a chance to internalize, to digest, to subject to inner working the pointers we are given through story and symbol. It is more. If we are right in thinking that the 'highest' form of prayer for the Kingdom is standing in all our weakness before God on the side of the poor and offering our psychic energies to confront evil in ourselves and in the cosmos, that very stance *requires* silence. It is such an effort, so demanding of our attention and our energy that we cannot simultaneously listen to what is being said or enter lustily into some song, be it never so 'appropriate'.

Some will say such prayer is for private endeavour only. 'Enter into your chamber and be still.' That, I suspect, is the giveaway. For to take that view seriously commits us to believing that public worship can never take us to the pinnacles of prayer. It may help us through the foothills, but will desert us once the going gets tough. That is palpable nonsense: we celebrate the Eucharist in public (and, nowadays, virtually never alone or in private). If we have communion with the Risen Christ in the company of Tom, Dick and Henrietta, we can expect to pray for his reign on earth in the same company.

And that company in its silence can be rich in its support and in its own symbolism. Silent, we are aware of each other and of our individual and corporate weakness. 'Sheep before the shearer' really are 'dumb'. They know they are held tight in a beneficient grip. Bleating is pointless. A congregation that is silent before its common Lord and Shepherd may find a depth of prayerfulness that will surprise it. If it is constantly bleating, it may be because it is unaware of the grip of the shepherd.

Sacrament

In this section I want to concentrate on only one sacrament, the Eucharist. It is the centre of the liturgy in most main-stream traditions and is so relevant to our theme that it must be accorded all the available space. I want to argue that the Eucharist is the epitome of political spirituality, but that it has been the object of the institutionalizing castration which we encountered again and again in the review of the biblical material in chapters 5 to 7. I shall concentrate on only four elements of the Eucharist, though the points I want to make could be applied equally well to elements I will not mention – for example, confession and absolution, intercession, the ministry of the word and the passing of the peace.

Let us start then with the offertory: the placing on the altar by the people through the priest of their offerings of money, bread and wine. Here is a deeply political as well as a deeply religious act. The collection of money, traditionally for the poor, not only has deep biblical and theological roots, but also has a symbolic load that raises many of the key Kingdom issues directly. We cannot explore them in detail here, but they include the gratuity of the Kingdom ('freely have you received, freely give . . .'), notions of the commonwealth of creation, the lordship of God over all creation, and the justice of economic life and relationships. Ritualized and commercialized out of all recognition, the collection has become more of an embarrassing intrusion into our psalmody than an acted parable of the nature of the Kingdom and the longing of the King for a loving response.

It is the other two elements of the offertory that are even more interesting, however. A member of the people of God offers bread. Bread is the symbol of work, of everyday commerce. And that symbol is taken to the Lord's table. Perhaps I can best communicate the lost significance of this by a story. In a Norfolk village lived a large landowner. He lived very comfortably on the rents from his farms and cottages. Over the years he acquired the reputation of being a hard landlord, constantly forcing up rents even though farm incomes were falling, evicting tenants who fell in arrears, refusing to compensate adequately for improvements, and failing to repair his cottages. As mechanization spread, he took in hand more and more of his farms and threw out of work many of the farm workers. . . . Sunday by Sunday, in the name of all the people in the village, he placed the symbol of work and economic life on the Lord's table.

A long time ago? Yes, perhaps. But translate it into today's terms, and see ourselves in that landlord. We maintain economic structures that deprive our fellow countrymen of work, housing, adequate medical care and a decent education; and that deprives millions in the rest of the world of freedom from starvation and oppression – and week by week we put the bread of economic life on the Lord's table and ask him to bless it and transform it into his flesh. And we do not even glimpse the enormity of what we do. Perhaps as a defence, we shut our inner eye so that it may not see the depth of the forgiveness we need or the radicality of the new life we are offered.

Wine is a symbol of leisure, of fun, pleasure, laughter, gaiety. Leave aside the meretricious and exploitative nature of much that passes for pleasure: confine the argument to leisure. The economy of leisure is no less in need of transformation than the economy of work. For the fact that I have as much leisure as I do, and of the quality that I do, is not unrelated to its denial to others – whether they be here in Britain, where the low-paid have to work excessive overtime, or whether they be in Asia or Latin America, where sweatshops producing for export markets have long been condemned by the International Labour Organization. Further, the fact that I can enjoy leisure is related to the fact that I work. To an unemployed person, leisure is a meaningless or even offensive concept. As long as I tolerate a system of economic management that regards unemployment as inevitable – which is tantamount to an economics that assumes people do not matter – I am obliged to see that leisure is a privilege enjoyed by some and denied to others.

When we offer wine, then, we are offering a political order in need of transformation. We are bringing our everyday way-of-doing-things (which is what politics is) face to face with ultimate reality – in the hope and expectation that it will be changed beyond recognition. This surely is the context *within which* our normally individualized understanding of the sacrament has to be set. Inner growth of the individual cannot be divorced or insulated from the society which conditions, even defines, that individual. Both are in need of the transforming power of love – which is why wine is so powerful a symbol.

With that in mind, we turn to the second element of the

Eucharist: the re-presentation, in the prayer of consecration, of the passion and resurrection of Christ. It would be inappropriate to review the whole theology of the passion in an essay like this; rather I select one indicative feature at the heart of the liturgy. The celebrant offers the bread and the wine, using the words of the institution: 'Do this . . .' What, it is fair to ask, do we think 'this' is that we are being instructed to 'do' – and which we would claim we are 'doing' Sunday by Sunday, celebration by celebration?

Notice first that a more accurate translation of the Greek is 'do these things'. What, then, are 'these things'? In the context of the Last Supper, they are clear. Jesus takes bread and wine, symbols as we have already seen, that have both secular and religious meanings. Bread is *both* common work *and* life itself. Wine is *both* leisure *and* saving life-blood. He takes these symbols, offers them for blessing to God the Father, and then breaks the bread. That is a crucial juxtaposition. For the offering-for-blessing is a dedication, a giving in service to the highest calling of the Father. And that calling is followed immediately by breaking. For it is only in breaking that sharing becomes possible. Take. Offer. Break. Give. Those are the 'things' that we do – and we do them with the symbols of our common life *and* of the life of Christ. At the point of 'these things', those – our life and his – are indistinguishable, so total is their interpenetration. And that is the proclamation of the Kingdom.

For the Kingdom comes when common work and common leisure are seized and dedicated to the highest calling of the Father. That calling will certainly involve the 'breaking' of any earthly system that is not totally interpenetrated with the life of Christ. It is only when it has thus been broken open that it can be shared with the poor, the vulnerable and the excluded. That breaking open is, however, not political or institutional vandalism: the point of the cross is that the breaking is an act of self-offering love. ' . . . My body given for you' is an invitation to give and break and share the common work and leisure of the mundane world, precisely in order to share it in a way that sustains and nourishes the people of the Kingdom.

On this account, then, the breaking of the bread is a deeply political as well as a deeply religious act. It is the symbol of how completely the one belongs to the other. It is the proclamation of the promise that 'these things' of self-offering love are the stuff of the Kingdom.

In the same way, 'take and eat this in remembrance that Christ died for you' is an invitation to a living memory that 'Christ died for you *all*'. Christ died for the whole cosmos, and the Kingdom involves the establishment of the reign of God over the whole cosmos. We share in his life – by eating his body – as both a first fruit of that cosmic redemption and as an enabling challenge to bring it alive in the everyday life of our world.

I hope this quick sketch suffices to demonstrate the political implications of the most solemn part of the Eucharist. I do not intend to dwell on how far removed they are from the consciousness of most of us: we are all the victims of a largely unconscious smothering of the political teeth of the Eucharist, itself part of a well established but wholly damnable tradition. It is not insignificant that when small groups of Christians have rediscovered those teeth and allowed them to bite, they have been persecuted, rejected and abused. Late nineteenth-century Britain; early twentieth-century Ireland and contemporary Brazil, South Africa and Philippines will afford examples. There are some signs that in the United States (but not, I fear, the United Kingdom) the politics of the Eucharist may re-emerge from the institutional cocoon: no doubt the familiar pattern of persecution, rejection and abuse will be re-enacted.

The consecrated bread and wine are then distributed to the people. They are often invited to 'feed on' Christ. Two points need to be emphasized. First, from the very earliest days of the Church's celebration of the Eucharist, it has seemed important to observe the principle that 'each has enough'. St Paul had harsh things to say about those who made pigs of themselves at the common meal (which may have been, or included, the Eucharist; or it may have been an agape) while others went hungry. The insistence on equality of distribution irrespective of social rank, ecclesiastical seniority or service record stems less from polite convention than from a proper understanding of what the distribution of the Body and Blood represents – the transformative possibilities of the life, death and resurrection of Christ. The

Kingdom is one where each has enough and none has excess: and the first fruits of the Kingdom reflect that.

The German theologian Ulrich Duchrow has made the point like this:

> Sitting around the table for the Lord's Supper are twelve Christians. Eight of them are coloured (black, brown, yellow, red, mixed race) and four of them are white. On the table there is rice, vegetables and chicken. Three whites (for there is also a small minority among the whites who are poor) and one coloured (the elite which co-operates with the whites in the poor countries) start the meal by taking all the chicken, most of the vegetables and most of the rice. All that remains for the seven coloured and the one white are some unequal portions of rice and some left-overs, so that some of them remain hungry. After the meal, the remains from the plates of the three whites and the one coloured are thrown away. The rich also have wine with their meal, the others only the small cup of wine at the Lord's Supper which follows the meal.

Second, the distribution of the elements is a process of feeding, of nourishment with the life of Christ. That is almost universally seen as a kind of personal store of soul-food to be drawn on in emergencies – like squirrels in a hard winter. Without rejecting the validity of that interpretation, we can see how inadequate an account it is in the light of the biblical material we reviewed earlier. For to 'feed on Christ' is to be identified with his life – and his life is the act that proclaims the Kingdom. His life offers the love that changes water into wine, that raises the dead, that heals the sick, that tells the poor, the persecuted and the mourner that they are in the right place. To 'feed on Christ' is to be caught up in the same quality of love; to be, in other words, a sign of the Kingdom. And that of course requires our own transformation; but it is a requirement that has a larger end in view than our personal salvation. The squirrel may well need his nuts, but he needs them to give him energy to change the world.

There is a hint of that in prayers that conclude the Eucharist in most traditions. 'Go in peace to love and serve the Lord.' We offer ourselves to be a 'living sacrifice', 'to live and work to thy praise and glory . . .' The formulations naturally vary, but even those traditions that use free prayer normally end the liturgy with the idea of self-offering in thanksgiving. It follows from what I have said so far that the dismissal of the people of God is a release into the world of a charge – a spiritual charge but also a political charge. If the people of God have entered into the reality of the Eucharist; if they have seen the world broken and given; if they have identified their lives with that of Christ and allowed them to be transformed in the process, they do not return to their community, their house or office as neutral, unprotesting participants in a world that denies the gratuity of the Kingdom. To do so would be to live in two worlds – a religious world and a 'real' world. And that is the process of disintegration. We are back with Legion and the need for healing. . . . The reality, of course, is that the Church is so careful to disguise the inner significance of the Eucharist, to file its teeth till they could not bite a milk-sop, that there is no danger of disintegration. Led to believe that the Eucharist is no more than a way in which the Lord nourishes the individual soul for its own particular inner journey to some mystical state of union with the Godhead, we people of God 'go' peacefully enough. . . . But we go with precisely the wrong kind of peace: the peace that lives comfortably with the *status quo*.

I am well aware that this is a cheap chapter to write and a costly one to live. It is one thing to describe some ways in which liturgy may be made more alert to the Kingdom themes of the Bible; it is quite another to introduce and implement changes in a worshipping community that has been reared on a blander diet. Can we pray the Kingdom without dividing the Church?

This could take us into deep and troubled water, for it raises traditional questions about the nature of the Church, and the relationship between the institutional Church and the true Church. In one form or another these questions have bothered Christians since the first century. Rather than explore them here, I shall end this chapter on a pragmatic note. What can be done to hold a worshipping community together as the liturgy is allowed to become more sensitive to the Kingdom issues? Here are some simple ground rules. (If they seem too simple, in my experience they are honoured more in the breach.)

First, a sustained teaching ministry, deeply rooted in the biblical record (and if possible the history of the Church) is a *pre*-requisite. As I have suggested implicitly thus far, however, that teaching has to be experiential and affective, and not just intellectual. Encouraging the whole community to do some of the exercises I have described (or variants of them), and discuss amongst themselves what they have learnt and what they have felt, is at least as important as filling them up with learning like so many empty milk bottles. Leadership of the learning process has to be shared, for no one has a monopoly of insight or feeling. Once people feel comfortable with each other and confident in their own ability to cope with the exercise, the richness and wisdom of the people will become apparent – wisdom often hitherto unsuspected and/or ignored. You will be – as I constantly am – humbled by how much you can learn from it.

Second, establish early on that just as nobody has a monopoly of insight, so no one 'answer', no particular 'response' to a biblical story or contemporary experience is exclusive. God shows us different bits of our own psyches, and different bits of his purposes of love. Intolerance of the experiences of others as they make their journey reveals an ignorance about prayer and the spiritual life.

Third, it is usually helpful if the 'stories' of members of the community can be shared. Those stories may be simple autobiographies or a full faith-history. Some people find it hard to talk about themselves even among people they know and trust. (Others find it hard *not* to talk about themselves.) The point is to ensure that members see each other as whole people. That will not necessarily prevent destructive projection of A's inner fears and difficulties on to B when B says something A finds threatening or distasteful, but it will reduce the impact of that projection and make disagreement easier to handle.

Fourth, it is obviously vital to avoid, especially early in the process, the kinds of pseudo-prayer for the Kingdom I described in chapter 3. Once the impression is gained that prayer for the Kingdom implies membership of this political party or that, it is best to abandon the whole enterprise. (Prayer may well change political attitudes and party affiliations. It will be surprising if it does not. But let it happen that way round.)

Fifth, informal liturgical experiment in small groups is often very creative. Those experiments will emerge spontaneously from the shared experience of the groups. My (not-all-that extensive) experience is again that there are gushing springs of liturgical creativity among the people of God; indeed a yearning to be allowed to express their deeper selves in their liturgical lives. Some of these experiments will be a triumphant success; some will be the reverse. That does not matter. What is important is that people learn that liturgy is a way of conveying truth, feeling, insight; that it is a living creative possibility, not a finely choreographed mime in a morgue.

Sixth, in line with what we were thinking about earlier in this chapter, encourage people to look around them – for stories, for symbols, for signs of the Kingdom, for God at work, especially in a 'secular' world. The temptation to divide world and Church goes astonishingly deep: disintegration again. It might be an idea to ban for a time any contribution that starts from 'within the Church'.

Seventh, consistent with points 5 and 6, it is important to ensure that any change in the formal liturgy comes from the whole people and reflects their reality. That implies making sure that everyone understands what that reality is and why the changes are being introduced to reflect it.

Eighth, try to avoid being over-solemn. Jesus had a great sense of humour and a no less great sense of fun. That does not seem to stop us proclaiming the life of Christ by boring each other to death. The coming of the Kingdom is a hard, painful business – which makes it the more important to enjoy what bits of the journey we can. More strategically, laughter is the best solvent of tensions and nascent animosities.

Ninth, it is hard but crucial to avoid an inner core of spiritual activists taking the show over and effectively excluding others, however unintentionally. Naturally some members of the community will be more willing than others to put in the time and work involved. Those who choose not to give the time must not be given the opportunity to dismiss the group that does as a clique or an exclusive minority.

Tenth and last, and in some ways most important, ensure that every member of the community sees the need for private prayers to accompany both group work and liturgy. It is a three-legged stool. Private prayer should include time for prayer for the whole community as well as for the individual and the world. For if the community is going to run into conflict and division as it begins to live and pray the Kingdom, it will need the prayers of its members.

Despite these hints, incomplete as they are, it will be unusual if the community does not experience centrifugal forces as it deepens its prayer for the Kingdom. That should neither surprise nor dismay us. Jesus warned his disciples of it more than once, and it has been the constant experience of the Church. The greatest threat is not posed by those who leave. The greatest threat is the temptation to self-righteousness of those who stay. For that is a sure sign that whatever their rhetoric and however striking their actions, their prayer for the Kingdom has degenerated into pseudo-prayer. They have become part of the problem.

9

Prayer and action

It is time to draw this book together. We started by trying to understand how many Christians, looking at the world in which they find themselves, are struck by two overwhelming emotional responses. They feel guilty. And they feel powerless. We surmised that this twin response produces one of two possible behavioural reactions – a total switch-off (often accompanied by a drift into an entirely individualized religion) or a pathological hyperactivism designed to purge the guilt and disprove the powerlessness.

We reflected that all of these conditions are connected with an unwillingness to take seriously prayer for the coming of the Kingdom. We defined that as standing in all our weakness before God on the side of the poor, and offering our psychic energies in the great battle against evil in ourselves, in our environment and in the whole cosmos. We saw Mary at the foot of the cross as a 'type' of that prayer, and compared elements of her watching-in-love with pseudo-prayer that can mislead or damage.

In preparation for prayer we looked at the role of story and did some preliminary fantasy exercises on secular stories, before spending rather longer on biblical stories that proclaim the great themes of the Kingdom – God's longing and love for his people, his offer of that love, its rejection, reoffering and enablement.

Because the institutionalization of the offer of the Kingdom seems to have been so recurrent but so destructive a feature of man's groping to come to terms with the offer of the Kingdom, we spent a little time in the last chapter thinking how the liturgical life of the Church could be enabled to make that offer more clearly and more attractively.

Now it would be a fair criticism of the story so far, you

145

may think, that we have sidestepped a central issue – the relationship between prayer and action. If I say my prayers properly, am I excused any further action? We have in fact picked this question up a time or two, and quickly put it down again. Some of the stories, both secular and biblical, had much emphasis on action: remember Cathy and Flora and, perhaps most marked, the parable of the seed. And in discussing the liturgy in the last chapter we thought about stories from the local situation – stories, that is, of the Kingdom in action. This last chapter carries this discussion further.

I shall make my standpoint clear from the outset. There can be no spirituality without action, without politics. I realize that may sound extreme. I was recently interviewed by my bishop, who wanted to know what I am intending to do now that I am unemployed. I told him I felt that I was being called to a ministry that combined theology, spirituality and politics. There was a long pause: 'I can think of a place that does the first two very well: but the third . . . that doesn't seem to feature on the agenda.'

Without going over the ground again, I hope it has become clear that prayer for the Kingdom is a political statement. I argued that to break the eucharistic bread is a political act, because it re-presents the breaking of earthly power-systems in preparation for a sharing of the Body of Christ. I argued that prayer for the Kingdom is a matter of taking sides; of committing our spiritual energies on the side of the poor against the forces of evil. And I argued that the Kingdom is to be lived; and it is given to those who try to live it.

If prayer for the Kingdom points ineluctably to the proper integration of spirituality and politics, it points no less clearly to mission – a word that falls uncomfortably on modern ears but is a convenient shorthand for the proclamation of the good news, not only to the poor and vulnerable, but also – and this is perhaps no less uncomfortable to the radical activists – to the rich and powerful. The coming of the Kingdom foresees a total transformation of the cosmos. That could, no doubt, be wrought by one creative act of God. It seems more likely that he prefers it to be wrought by the willing co-operation of (a majority of ?) his people. To use another vocabulary, 'Kingdom issues' cannot be lived apart from 'mission issues', for the one implies the other in a repetition of the theme of mutual interpenetration: the central point is that as prayer for the Kingdom issues in political action, so it also issues in missionary or evangelistic action.

The implication is obvious. The political action and the evangelistic action are related; they spring from the same root. Ideally they are identical, as I hinted in the stories of chapter 4. Where the Kingdom is lived courageously and prophetically, it will 'judge' the powers of the world by revealing their narrowness and inadequate conception of gratuity; but it will also proclaim the nature of the good news that Christ is bringing his people. At its best, the peace movement is an example of that identity. It reveals the misconception of the sources, even the very nature, of security as held by the defence authorities; and by pointing to an order of harmony and justice it proclaims, albeit incompletely, some of the leading themes of the Kingdom.

Let us, however, try to be a little more systematic about the relationship between spirituality (in its popular, narrow and misleading sense), politics and mission. We have seen how the one interpenetrates the other. To put that more dynamically, it is a dialectic relationship, wherein the one acts upon the other and transforms both itself and the other. The classic example of dialectic is the Hegelian thesis, antithesis and synthesis, where the thesis and antithesis react upon each other and are transcended in the synthesis. Light, dark and colour are more prosaic examples.

The relationship between prayer, politics and mission is dialectic in this sense at four levels: the individual, the local, the structural, and the cosmic; a word on each of these.

Prayer, politics and mission interact at the individual level. Prayer 'informs' or permeates my political stances and instincts, gradually drawing me from a politics that puts my interests at the centre and subjects all other interests to my own. Rather it releases me from an egocentric politics to the politics of gratuity, forgiveness and trust. At the same time, however, my political journey 'informs' my prayers, by allowing me to bring new material imaginatively alive in my prayer life – stories again. As my political stances are changed by what I discover in prayer of the love of God, so my ability to live and proclaim the nature of the Kingdom is changed.

And that is evangelism. Now as these three react upon each other, so I as a person am changed; and as I am changed so I act as an agent of change in every environment in which I am active. This 'synthesis' is not one final state: it is not like baking a cake. It is not the case that once you have mixed the ingredients and left it in the oven for a period, that is that. Except in some sense of final sanctification, we are, rather, constantly engaged in a journey. Any synthesis is provisional and transitory. As soon as we begin to feel comfortable at one level of synthesis, we are, as it were, given a further shove and sent off down the helter-skelter of deepening prayer, more radically open politics, more hopeful proclamation. The role of suffering in administering that shove is crucial – as we have repeatedly discovered throughout this book.

I have put the journey in highly individualized terms – my prayer, my politics, my proclamation. I make no apologies for that: indeed I want to emphasize that both the starting and finishing points of the helter-skelter are points at which I have to look afresh at my own inwardness. My prayer will infect my politics as it infects my innermost self and my conscious understanding of that self. Both prayer and politics will infect my proclamation as I – the real, deep-down me rather than ·the carefully cultivated public persona – am changed by the grace of the Spirit. To try to drive a psychological or spiritual wedge between this inner growth and outer activity is to court all the problems of disintegration so familiar to Legion.

Having said that, we need to balance it by returning to the three other stages on which we all act, what I called earlier the local, the structural and the cosmic. It is on those stages that we live out or exhibit what is going on inwardly. Indeed it is only when we are on those stages that our politics and our proclamation mean anything: and that implies it is only then that the wholeness of our prayer, even our most silent, inward prayer, is properly honoured.

By the 'local' stage, I mean what I have called elsewhere in this book 'our place'; where we have standing, the right to speak and perhaps the right to be heard. That may be our family, our community, our Church, our office, school or factory. The dialectic of prayer, politics and proclamation operates there, in 'our place'. The call to gratuity, justice and peace is as real in the home (and sometimes, it seems, as costly) as it is anywhere else; and the need to proclaim the good news to the broken, the mourning and the desperate may be as pressing at our table or in our street as it is on the stage of the world. It follows, then, that 'our place' will furnish our prayers with relevant material, ready for the transforming touch of the Spirit.

The 'structural' refers to the level at which we are all caught up in structures and relationships over which we have little control, and from which we nonetheless may profit, as we saw in chapters 1 and 2. This 'stage' overlaps with 'our place': a family is both a structure and a set of relationships that generates its own problems and possibilities. The structural stage extends, however, from the micro-structure of the family or the office to macro-structures such as the international economy or NATO. In each of these, the same dialectic of prayer, politics and proclamation can – and, I would argue, should – operate. In prayer we stand alongside the victims of international economic injustice; in politics we identify with their interests; and in proclamation we 'exhibit' the Kingdom of gratuity where their concerns are taken as seriously as anyone else's. The dialectic forces us into an even deeper commitment until we reach some kind of ultimate where we *know* experientially the coming of the Kingdom.

That kind of knowing, of apprehension of the utterness of God's care for his creation has already taken us on to the final stage, the cosmic. Past, present and future; animate and inanimate – the whole of Creation is caught up in the final triumphant synthesis of prayer, politics and proclamation. That synthesis does not ignore or overlook the pain and anguish of a world in torment.

It takes them as both starting and finishing points. In her 'thirteenth showing' or vision, Julian of Norwich, a warm and tender woman as well as a great mystic, says: 'Our Lord brought to my mind all things that are not good . . . all the bodily and spiritual pains and passions of his creatures.' She was reminded, she says, of 'the utter stripping he accepted for us in this life', and reflected that 'We are all stripped and shall be . . . until we are stripped . . . of all our inner desires that are not wholly good.' And when she wondered why those 'inner desires that are not wholly good' or, in a 'stark word, sin' had not been prevented in creation – 'for then, I thought, all should have been well' – Jesus told me all that I needed: "Sin is behovely – it had to be. But all shall be well, and all shall be well, and all manner of things shall be well." '